D0897897

AMERICA'S SHAME AND REDEMPTION

DWIGHT LOWELL DUMOND

AMERICA'S SHAME and REDEMPTION

DWIGHT LOWELL DUMOND

NORTHERN MICHIGAN UNIVERSITY PRESS
MARQUETTE, MICHIGAN

Manufactured in U.S.A.
THE BOOK CONCERN, PRINTERS, HANCOCK, MICH.

FOREWORD

The summer of 1965 at Northern Michigan University will long be remembered as the summer when Dr. Dwight L. Dumond, Professor Emeritus of History at the University of Michigan, became our first Distinguished Visiting Professor.

Dr. Dumond is a master teacher, thorough scholar, and stimulating speaker. He is recognized as one of the world's foremost authorities on the history of the Civil War and the issues and effects of slavery in the United States.

History comes alive through Dr. Dumond's pen and voice. Reflected in his series of seven lectures entitled "Wooden Spoons," are a lifetime of study and research, a belief in the dignity and natural rights of man, and a concern for the well-being of all people in a world of conflicting and shifting values.

Dr. Dumond touched the lives of students, faculty, and citizens of the Marquette community during his residency on our campus. It is with great pride that Northern Michigan University publishes his lectures in book form so that others may share the rich experience of a brilliant and memorable summer with Dr. Dwight L. Dumond — dedicated teacher, perceptive historian, and thoughtful American.

Edgar L. Harden

PRESIDENT

NORTHERN MICHIGAN UNIVERSITY

CONTENTS

INTRODUCTION

This is the land of liberty and of oppression; a land of good will and of hate. We love the beautiful lady in New York Harbor but hang our heads in shame at our infidelity. We pride ourselves upon public schools and close them to millions of children. We buy friendship abroad with our dollars and lose prestige by our cruelties and injustices at home. We want to provide leadership for the moral forces of the world but murder two of our greatest Presidents. All this and more, we do because of color. We call it prejudice which means nothing. We call it racialism, but it is not that in a strict sense, nor is it color entirely. It is the survival of slavery which was and is the subordination to the white population of millions of people, a portion of whose ancestors were slaves and of African descent.

The slaves were brought here from Africa, directly or by way of the West Indies. White men were not satisfied to let them produce their own children, and before long there were hundreds of thousands of persons of Irish-African, English-African, German-African, French-African, or Dutch-African origin. The African side of such unions was almost always, but not quite, on the mother's side, so slaveholders quickly passed laws saying that children followed the status of the mother. Thousands of the slaves after a while were of fairer complexion than many whites. That fact helped a good many slaves to escape, made fools of lawmakers and courts who said color was a presumption of slavery, and put every person with a dark skin in danger of being seized as a fugitive slave. When slaves were set free, the states kept them in the submerged class by saying a trace of Negro blood made them Negro and forbade them to marry a white person.

The entire history of human relations in this country has been one of a constant battle against the idea that people of color are inferior to whites. Out of that idea have come a thousand malign influences to wither aspiration and hope. Once society begins to sort people out into categories on the basis of bodily characteristics, family background, religious beliefs, or occupations, people begin to make false judgments, and more important, to dislike and hate people instead of disagreeing with their ideas. Then we get despised minorities, denial of equality, injustices, discrimination, and trouble. We have heard persons say a thousand times that people of color are ignorant. It is not true of course, but the frightening thing is that such persons never think about ignorance in white men who go to the ballot-box or even seek high office. It is only when ignorance is clothed in a dark skin that they take notice, and the ignorance and the skin are often confused in their minds.

Hate begets hate. Confusion on the part of men of color is rapidly merging into hatred of their oppressors, and hate long continued spells death for everyone. It plunged us into a long and devastating Civil War; it cost us the lives of two of our greatest Presidents; and it has brought us again to the verge of bloodshed and revolution. How much more do we have to pay in heartaches and blood and empty chairs before we cleanse our minds and souls of this terrible sickness. American history is going to turn upon our ability to meet this challenge, for with nations as with individuals it is character that counts. As people live, and love or hate, so will the national character take shape.

If we can not listen to the voice of truth; if we can not be shocked out of our indifference by the lynchings, the bombings, and the riots; if we can not see the signs of impending disaster which crowd in upon us; then bloodshed is as certain as anything in this world ever was certain. We can no longer have peace in the presence of such enormous iniquity. Human rights can not be compromised. Compromise means surrender of something and man can not give up what God has bestowed upon him, and what his ancestors have purchased with their blood; not life, nor liberty, nor honor and self-respect.

Here is the acid test of democracy. If we save democratic institutions, it will have to be on the basis of equality of human rights. A democratic society may have majorities and minorities on questions of public policy. They are inevitable and ever changing, but it can not have majorities and minorities on the basis of human attributes. It must rejoice in individual differences. It must treat people as individuals. It must listen to the cry of the poor and oppressed, if not through love, then through fear, for it has the power to destroy.

As a historian I have been distressed by the lack of an intellectual ferment comparable to the Revolutionary period which produced the finest literature extant in the science of government; or comparable to the pre-Civil War period of reform and Christian benevolence which produced the most powerful arguments ever written in defense of of human rights. Now we are at the crossroads. We are beginning to get an intellectual ferment and some literature. Some statesmen, some preachers, some newspaper editors of eloquence are displaying strong interest in the improvement of human relationships, but there is so much to be done and so little time.

As a teacher I have been lifted up in spirit by the response of our young people. They were born into a world of confusion, of hate, of fear, when war seemed inescapable and untimely death inevitable. They grew up in a generation that was starved in mind and soul, confused by irrational hatreds, and unable to think of any kind of security except atomic bombs. No one seemed interested in improving human relationships. This did not make sense to them, any part of it.

They had the spirit of youth and daring and vision. They saw beyond the narrowing horizon what clouded vision had denied their elders. They saw the opportunity to build a new world on the basis of service, of equality of all peoples, of justice and peace. Nationalism, racialism, religion had no place in it. We do not think that history will say we were wrong in this judgment. They found a leader, a Moses to take them out of a wilderness of intellectual depravity over into the promised land—the world of their dreams.

John F. Kennedy had the love and affection and trust of more young people than any other man ever elected to the Presidency of this country. Why? Because he combined all of those qualities which mean so much to these young people of ours who want to go on living, and to fulfill the destiny of man. He had the courage of romance. He had the intellectual power of a disciplined mind. His faith in Divine guidance had the force of triumph and conviction. He loved his fellow men. He wanted peace. So great was his personal prestige and the power of his position throughout the world that four more years may well have given youth complete fulfillment of its golden dreams.

But we would not have it. Hate struck him down as it had struck down Lincoln and driven Wilson to his grave by the loss of his cause. The kind of hate that comes from generations of sucking at the wrinkled teats of outworn creeds. The kind that comes from hating Negroes, and hating Catholics, and hating Jews, and hating the authority of the Federal government and the Supreme Court. The kind that comes from hating the poor because they make us uncomfortable, and the working man because he too wants a home and an automobile and a good education for his children. He might have saved us, but we killed him in the fullness of our anger, our bigotry, our fanaticism, and the hearts of our youth are full of grief and their eyes are filled with tears. They have rallied again, and I am convinced their faith is as strong and their vision as clear as that of the young men and women who saved us in the days of the nation's greatest trial. It is to them, and particularly to those who sat in my classes through the years and whom I love so much, that these lectures are dedicated.

I

GUIDELINES OF AMERICAN HISTORY

A long way and a long time from here and now, two young men from foreign lands sat talking with death not far away for one. He was a veteran from the first of Kitchener's armies, a young man from Cambridge, and he was talking not about himself but about certain ideas, currently being expressed by men of his country, offensive to our common notion of what the war was about, to which or to whom he applied the term "wooden spoons." We, in the United States today, are well supplied with wooden spoons, fashioned by a generation of historians who failed to deal with moral values.

We have had in this country since the days of European penetration a contest between the philosophy of human rights and the philosophy of arbitrary power for control of the nation. It is a contest for survival of intellectual and moral accountability, for the right and responsibility of every person to do what is required by reason and conscience in his relationship to others and to God, for the equality of all men in the endowment of rights, the security of rights, and the exercise of rights.

The first sentence of our Declaration of Independence was a prospectus of this democratic philosophy. We wanted freedom to shape our own destiny as a people. We said to all the peoples of the world that all men are created equal; not black men, or white men, or red men, but all men. Millions of people have a false concept of the term equality. This is the first of our wooden spoons. We meant that all men have the capacity to think, and remember, and reason; that they possess the same emotions, the same passions, the same power to choose and to act by choice; that they can tell the difference between right and wrong, have standards of morality, and are responsible to society and to God for the way they behave; that all have the same origin, the same rights, and the same responsibilities. Deny this equality and all the defenses of freedom fall like a house of cards.

Then we wrote our first Constitution—the Articles of Confederation—deliberately, knowingly, and purposely leaving out all reference to the color of a man's skin, hair, or eyes, and place of origin. Then we wrote our second Constitution (1787) saying no man could be deprived of his life, liberty or property without due process of law. No man ever has or ever will find mention of color in the basic documents of this country. No man can find or state any argument for his own freedom which does not apply in the same way and to the same degree to every other man. No man can find any evidence, any argument, any precedent to show that any person stands before the throne of God or the bar of justice on any other basis than equality with every other person. That is the basis on which we founded our government and established our democratic institutions. Three times since then freedom-loving men and women have been compelled to rally to the defense of human rights. Ultimate victory is a moot question. The courage of the handful of men and women who marshaled the hosts against slavery and who labor now by night and day to suppress the flames of civil strife should be our glory forever; yet not one person in a thousand knows their names and those who died to save the nation and to strike the chains of slavery from millions of our people are almost forgotten in every community from which they came. In 1833, in the famous trial of Prudence Crandall in Connecticut for opening her private school to Negro girls, the prosecutor, Andrew Judson, said: "It was a nation of white men who formed and have administered our government, and every American should indulge that pride and honor, which is falsely called prejudice, and teach it to his children. Nothing else will preserve the American name, or the American character." That statement has seldom been equalled for downright bigotry and falsification but millions of people endorse it today. It is another of our wooden spoons.

It is the duty of government to watch over and protect men's rights. There are a lot of depraved people in this country. It is one of the sad features of human nature. They are scheming, deceitful, cunning, cruel. They hurt other people who are weaker than themselves or they join with others of their kind and gang up on defenseless people. That is why we have governments and laws, to protect persons who need protection, otherwise we would have perpetual chaos. The task of government is easy if people have a strong sense of justice and morality, difficult if they are indifferent, if their sense of justice is corrupted, or if they have contempt for poor, unfortunate persons or those of a different religion or skin color. Let those kinds of people gain control of the government and use it to persecute instead of protect, or let them gain enough power in the government to keep it from its primary function of protection, and that country is on its way to everlasting destruction. They have done both in the United States.

We set the stage perfectly for this when we framed the Constitution. We did not abolish slavery. We did not even provide for the protection of the slaves, or for a sanctuary to which they might flee, or for any possibility of ultimate freedom. What we did do was create a powerful aristocracy: a privileged class with unprecedented powers. These men were given political power in the Federal government in direct proportion as they owned slaves. That power was great enough to control Congress, the Presidency, and the Courts because it was based upon privilege. These men worshipped at the shrine of slavery, and when they entered the temple of freedom in Washington it was with undeviating and unquestioning dedication to the mores of the slave country, regardless of the best interests of the nation.

We allowed the state governments to control all relationships between masters and slaves. The slaveholders controlled the state governments, directly or indirectly, and the only laws dealing with slavery were for the protection of society and the special interests of slaveholders. That favored aristocracy popularized the idea that the slaves were biologically inferior to the master race, that the states were sovereign, that what was good for the slaveholders was good for the South, and that what was good for the South was good for the country. They even claimed it was good for the slaves. The slaveholding aristocracy was not one of noble descent, of immense landed possessions, of wealth and industry, but of white skins. Justice and equity could not survive except in a fragmentary way.

Hence we have had two great antagonistic forces in the nation from the earliest days. Slavery was not a mild, humane, benevolent institution, not in this country or any other. It deprived its victims of freedom to come and go as they wished, to read or write, to enjoy privacy, to marry, to own property, even the clothes on their backs. It robbed them of their manhood, of the protection of the law, of hope and ambition. It killed millions to enslave the few. It robbed the continent of Africa of its children, and then it beat them down into the dust, destroyed their minds, and killed their souls. Anyone could buy a slave in the flesh markets of this country. They were sold like horses and cows. He who bought could torture, whip, kill those who resisted him for any reason or ran away. He could use the women himself or hire them to others and he could break up families by sale. There was no limit to his power over these unfortunates among his fellow men. He held it by force, by fear, by permission of his state government and its laws.

This tragic business all started back in colonial days when greedy people without conscience, certainly without fear of God's retribution, began buying slaves from African slave traders. These traders made huge profits by selling human beings hunted down by themselves or someone else in Africa. They gave Africa alcoholic beverages and guns in return, kept the whole continent in riotous turmoil for four hundred years, turned the clock back to the days of medieval barbarism, and left millions of people politically disorganized and spiritually dispirited. This was an international, world-wide affair then and it is now.

Christians went to war, killed upon the battlefield,
Behaved much like the pagans from afar
In all things save they would not sell their captives
If they were members of the Christian church.
Fate such as that was held in sheer abhorrence,
Reserved for men who knew naught of the Christ
child,
The benefit of saving grace, the Sermon on the
Mount,
For men less skilled in war, less organized for peace,
For men whose skin belied all claims to membership
In Western, Christian nations.

King Henry had freed his slaves, but not Elizabeth.
That creature had herself a host of able men
Who sailed upon the seas and plundered ships for
gold,
Sold human flesh for gold, took calculated risks

To plant the British flag on lands across the sea,
Then stole young girls and boys—precious youth of
Africa,
Babes in arms, young mothers torn from brothers,
fathers,
Unoffending children of the living God, spared to
brand, breed and sell
As laborers like horses, donkeys, cattle
In the land of freedom.

The Dutch were guilty and the Spanish, Portuguese,
All Christian people too, seeking power, prestige,
Guilt knows no single home in matters such as this,
When men fall prey to force, supported by the law,
When Princes close their minds to prayers for
justice,
Fight wars to gain the power of exploitation,
The treaty rights to buy and sell whole continents,
Millions of distressed souls, consigned to living
death,
Deprived of their manhood, shorn of their right to
live
Except in degradation.

White skins and Christian faith, poor subtitutes for
law,
When men grew dark or light from sunshine or
from shade,
When nations rose and fell, nor long remained
secure,
When greed, lust, inhumanity, infamy without end
Respected not the bonds of Christian fellowship,
Nor age, nor sex, nor individuality

Of those too weak, obscure, without friends, position,
Far distant from their homes, beyond the pale of law,
Where slavers roamed at large.

The white men who brought these inoffensive people to America and those who bought and held them down were never free themselves afterward. They were victims of fear—fear that the slaves would rise up and slay them, fear that a greater authority than their state governments would take away their freedom to oppress, fear of a changing world. Fear is the mother of oppression, and fear destroyed their souls. Slavery made them poor in spite of all their efforts to grow rich from the sale of children. It made them cruel, callous, and ungodly. All of their fears, their determination to live by the profits of other men's labor, their love of luxury and ease turned them against the world. They did not permit and never would have permitted any loosening of the bonds of slavery or establishment of machinery to protect the slaves or promote emancipation.

What did they do? Everything they could to keep the slaves ignorant, depraved, docile; to keep those who hated slavery from saying why they hated it; to protect their power to enslave and oppress without interference from the national conscience, the national authority, and God Almighty. They said by law that children of slave mothers, regardless of what man begot them, were slaves when born. This gave them profits, stability, freedom to prey upon female slaves without loss. They said all persons of African origin were slaves whether or not they became Christians thus changing the basis of slavery from heathenism to color of man's skin. They said persons of African origin were biologically inferior to whites and incapable of making advancement if given an opportunity; that slavery was their natural status; that they were the embodiment of everything cowardly, indolent, and vicious in nature; and, having proclaimed the doctrine of racialism, they then starved the slaves mentally and spiritually to prove it. They imposed heavy penalties upon anyone who taught slaves to read or write, causing them to wander about as in a pit of darkness, without hope this side of the grave, without knowledge, and without right to make decisions or moral judgments. There is no glory to be found in the history of slavery, nor monuments to its achievements save proof of man's inhumanity to man. It was a house of death, a sepulcher of broken bodies and wasted souls. There never was and never will be inspiration to be derived from a ruined man. Slavery was born in the death cries of millions. The history of the African for four hundred years has been one of death, enslavement, denial of natural rights at the hands of Europeans and Americans. Our burden of sin is great, because war, slavery, and defilement of the human body are monumental sins.

Life was cheap in the slave country. It is cheap today. Lack of proper food, overwork, exposure to the elements, absence of medical care are notorious. The ordinary punishment was thirty-nine lashes with the cowhide whip or perforated paddle. They were administered on occasion by owner, any member of his family, overseer, the common jailer, members of a road patrol, or by anyone who had hired the slave's time and to whom such power was delegated. Fortunate indeed, and rare, was the slave among three and one-half million who had not been chastised. They were hunted by dogs when they ran away. They were branded with hot irons on the cheek, back, legs for purposes of identification. Sometimes ears were cropped or severed or teeth were knocked out for the same purpose. Many bore the marks of lacerated flesh or gunshot wounds. Many more were killed when resisting punishment or recapture. They were shackled with heavy irons; strung up by the thumbs or wrists with heavy weights upon their feet; spread-eagled upon the ground, many dying under the lash or of their wounds. Those who were incorrigible, who ran away, or were tired out suffered greatly; but, no less than in the African hunt itself, the old, worn out, diseased, blind, deaf and dumb, were handicaps to profit, not objects of tender care.

Slavery kept the South in ignorance. Slaveholders wanted it that way. They were an aristocracy, dangerously close to a caste. Education is the greatest counter-balance in the world to the endowment of wealth and birth. Emancipation of poor men from the power of an aristocracy depends upon it. The law forbade teaching slaves to read or write. It would have led straight to disquiet, insurrection, emancipation. It made no provision for education of free people of color. Education of these people, free or slave, would have proved the theory of racial inequality to be exactly what it was and still remains: the quintessence of insipidity. Only a fool would endorse the doctrine of racialism. It is a mythological concept, in its American origins a rationalization, in its survival a monstrous lie. No scholar would take it seriously, nor would anyone who respected the basic principles of religion, science, or history. James Madison, called the Father of the Constitution, declared: "We have seen the mere distinction of color, made in the most enlightened period of time, a ground of the most oppressive dominion ever exercised by man over man;" and more recently a distinquished biologist, Dean Charles G. Wilber, spoke truly when he said, "Unfair treatment based on racial differences is a sin—fundamentally because it denies a biological reality, and that reality is the basic, undeniable, scientific unity of humankind. The unfair treatment of any part of the human species is an affront to nature."

The Dignity of Man. The equality of all men. Government by consent of the governed. Dignity, equality, consent, here were the foundation principles of our democracy and the greatest of these was equality. Nothing ever will be quite settled until we accept it as the most important injunction of our daily lives, but where and how could these basic principles of democracy be reconciled with the philosophy of slavery and racialism? The answer is nowhere because under that philosophy no one ever could be secure and no one certainly free. It led to the proscription and exile of liberal preachers from the slave states. Anyone who questioned the righteousness of slavery in an area where slaveholders had consolidated their power was denounced as a traitor and incendiary. Then the slave power reached out to enforce silence in the nation. Holding high posts in educational institutions, churches, and government, they were able to do so. They centered their attack upon antislavery men and women. These great intellectuals, humanitarians, and statesmen would have been indicted for treason and hanged upon the scaffold had slaveholders been in the majority and had slavery not already been abolished in the Northern states. Rewards upward of $50,000 were offered and publicly subscribed for the delivery of many of them into the hands of Southern mobs. They were charged with the attemped overthrow of a venerable American institution. The slave states officially demanded the suppression of their organizations and publications by their states of residence. They claimed the right to extradite them and convict them for violations of the laws of the slave states. They forced publishing houses to delete references to slavery from school textbooks and magazines. They reached into the free states to incite mob violence against antislavery lecturers, editors, and free persons of color. They used their tremendous power in political parties to enforce party regular-ity and to discipline public officials of antislavery views. They forced gross violations of academic freedom upon college administrators. They made a mockery of freedom of the political press. They forced a gag into the throats of Congressmen, silencing all debate on slavery and sending forth to the world a studied defense of slavery and mob rule. They forbade United States postmasters to deliver antislavery literature and compelled them by state law to rifle the mails and destroy such literature. In short, they established for themselves alone the greatest of all monopolies: a monopoly of human rights.

In its totality, what happened constituted a great national disaster. Far too many people forsook the high principles on which our nation was founded, repudiated the philosophy of Christian liberalism, lost their sense of justice and equity, abandoned respect for due process of law, and allowed greed, ignorance, hate, pride, sadism to control their relations with others. Where there should have been love, they spread hatred. Where there should have been union, they sowed discord. Eventually a great sickness pervaded the land which was not cured by the blood-letting of the Civil War because it was a spiritual sickness. It did not suddenly come upon us. It had always been with us as a nation. It grew and grew until it took the form of social insanity. It was in that kind of atmosphere that sectionalism was born and flourished before 1860; and in that kind of atmosphere that it has grown stronger since that time.

"I am a citizen of Mississippi in the first place, a citizen of the beloved Southland in the second place, and a citizen of the United States in the last place." So wrote a local Methodist minister to a distinguished newspaper editor during the riots at Oxford. Here is a present day expression of decentralization as cunning in its deception as any since the days of the Machiavellian John C. Calhoun. Sectionalism always was and is a child-like faith in the habits and ideas of one's home town. Sometimes it reaches the level of a state or even a geographical area. It never is broad enough or comprehending enough to include the nation, or the interests of the nation, or the unity and security of the nation. It will not accept the Constitution of the United States, the authority of Congressional law, or the decisions of the Supreme Court, unless they conform to its own cross-roads philosophy and its own ill-manners toward other people. So far as people of color are concerned, it means sitting astride them because of their color. Slaves were victims of unrestrained sadism. Free persons of color were victims of incessant mortification. When those who suffered had the courage to assert their rights, they were cruelly punished, imprisoned, or delivered up to the tender mercies of the mob. Persons who spoke out against slavery and abuse of free persons of color, though they spoke with the voice of angels, were condemned as common brawlers and disturbers of the peace. Racists in the day of slavery and today have never hesitated to strike down the most talented men should they dare to lift their voices against the evil doctrine.

Sectionalists, who call themselves state rights men, will not pay any attention to what people in other parts of the country think or how they behave. It is local ignorance sneering at the idea of a national conscience. It moans and groans if anyone writes a book or a newspaper editorial or speaks on the radio or television suggesting there might be some grounds for criticism of its behavior at the present time or that of its ancestors now safely interred and beyond caring. It is ready to kill in defense of its infamy as well as its virtue, past, present, or future. It intimidates broadcasting companies and book publishers. It intimidates book sellers and librarians and school-teachers to keep such literature out of the hands of everyone. It intimidates politicians, and tries to intimidate Presidents, and Chief Justices, and Attorneys-General.

The men who founded this nation believed and said that promotion of the general welfare was a basic function of government, and so was promotion of national unity. They tried to make certain that every person would live and prosper under a government which drew its powers from the combined wisdom and the common desires of all the people. They did this by making the Constitution and the laws made under it the supreme law of the land. Those laws are made in full view of the entire country. They are scrutinized in the making by brilliant newspaper men, domestic and foreign correspondents, organizations especially designed to protect civil rights and national interests, high dignitaries of the churches, brilliant lawyers, and independent scholars.

State and local laws are framed in comparative obscurity, often by men who have never read anything but a local newspaper and whose vision extends a little beyond the next cornfield. These men are guided by local interest and local prejudice. They neither know nor care what is going on in the outside world. Yet the people in the state or local community who live under those laws are also citizens of the United States and sometimes citizens of another state in temporary residence. Millions of people in the United States are living in some state other than the one in which they were born and educated. They are citizens of the United States always and citizens of a state only if they happen to be living there.

Here is the source of much of our trouble today, and it is not going away of its own accord. Those people who move, and millions of people of color and white people both have moved from the lower South, have lived and been educated under the local laws, ordinances, and prejudices which will not let them eat, or pray, or go to school, or play, or use the libraries together. It is some business of other people that this is allowed to happen. The way in which people are taught to behave and allowed to behave is the business of the United States, of the people of the United States and their Congress and President. Whoever loses sight of the general welfare, whoever tries to subordinate national interest to local prejudice, is destroying the security of this country as surely as if he were a foreign enemy. The great strength of a nation lies in its moral power drawn from the whole of the people. The nation which has the greatest reserves of moral and intellectual power is the strongest nation. Its people must have the best education, complete freedom in cultural activities, no restraints upon their hopes and aspirations, and respect for the dignity and equality of each other as men and women and as citizens of the United States.

That was the promise of America, but we failed to live up to that promise. The men who framed the Constitution did not abolish slavery which enshrined the doctrine of racialism, and racialism spread like a cancer through all the vital organs of the nation. They gave men extra political power for owning slaves. They gave them the right to roam all over the country carrying people off to slavery as alleged fugitives and do so in complete violation of all the essentials of due process of law, and the men who profited thereby were determined to keep it that way. Free persons of color, and those white men who claimed the right to discuss slavery in peaceable assemblies, in churches, and in newspapers were set upon by howling mobs. Presidents, members of Congress, Federal and state judges, governors, mayors, editors of political newspapers, even some preachers joined the pagan onslaught. The guilt of mobs was charged to their victims. Mob violence was called an expression of public sentiment. Individual rights were held subordinate to social interest as determined by public sentiment at any time. Public officials stood silent or lent encouragement as mobs went about their work of destruction, claiming the rights of discretion in performance of duty.

All mobs are social monsters, conceived by sadists;
Born of hate, jealousy false pride, intemperance;
Roaming, moaning, mouthing blasphemy, slander, filth,
Raping, beating, whipping, stoning, burning, killing,
Destroying homes, schools, churches, printing presses,
Not in sudden passion, not with provocation—

By men whose hands are clean, whose hearts are black as night:
Men of wealth, power, position, influence, trust,
In their communities.

All of this has continued down to the present day. The Constitution allowed the states to retain the police powers under which slavery existed and under which people of color have been crucified for three hundred years. Congress allowed the states to retain absolute power over slaves and slavery. Slavery was an exercise of force by one man over another and by all white people over all people of color, recognized and sustained by state law. After a while the courts of the United States said that people of color were not citizens and that color was a presumption of slavery.

It was the extraordinary political power of the white people in slave states which allowed them to hold in contempt the authority of a constitutional majority in the nation and subordinate its authority to the laws of their own states. They bent the provisions of the Constitution to their own will by curious interpretations. John C. Calhoun, Jefferson Davis, William L. Yancey and a host of lesser people with more enthusiasm than brains said that the Constitution was a compact among sovereign states, and that a state, being sovereign, could declare an Act of Congress unconstitutional. Never was so much evil concealed in the cloak of virtue. The theory was that the majority in the nation could control the President, Congress, and the Supreme Court and thus trample upon and abuse the rights of a minority in the nation unless that minority through its control of a state government could declare an Act of Congress unconstitutional. The actuality was that they wanted power to protect their right to oppress minorities in their own states. It was power to oppress that they wanted, power to hold the people of color in subordination, slave or free, forever. Under the state sovereignty—state interposition—nullification—concurrent majority—call it what you like—theory of Calhoun and the South then and now, any state with scarcely enough people to make a decent city ward could keep the rest of the country from passing any kind of legislation in Congress. The idea of local autonomy in the nation was so contrary to constitutional government as to be beyond the pale of respectability, but so powerful was the determination to keep people of color in complete subordination forever that the doctrine of state sovereignty was carried to its logical conclusion of secession. Eleven states tried to break up the Union in 1860-61 to preserve slavery. They got so tangled up in the spider's web of their own weaving that they failed miserably and succeeded only in hastening the day of freedom for the slaves at a terrific cost of human lives.

They were able to bring the nation to this brink of disaster because political parties accommodated themselves to the demands of the slaveholders thoughout the whole of this period. They did not evade, neither did they compromise. Slavery expanded in area and in power, dominating the moral and political philosophy of the people of the slave states. The three-fifths rule gave them the margin of political power necessary to prevent positive action in Congress against slavery either for its melioration or containment. They never admitted the evil of slavery even as an abstraction, nor the possibility of abolishing it at some future time. They never admitted the power of Congress to abolish slavery in the District of Columbia or in the territories, or to refuse admission to a new slave state, or to abolish the interstate slave trade. They never admitted the citizenship of persons of color or their right to enter unmolested into a slave state. They had the power and they used it to restrain discussion by the gag rule in the House of Representatives, to intrude into the free states with a Congressional fugitive slave law, and to establish color both as a presumption of slavery and immutability of Negro inferiority as recognized principles in the Federal courts. They had the power and they used it to open all the territories to slavery. No! There was no compromise; only arrogance, aggression, ever new demands and new encroachments on the rights of man.

There is a gulf as deep as the ocean between the state rights philosophy of old Virginia—Jefferson, Ritchie, Taylor,—and that of Calhoun, Davis, and Yancey. These earlier men would never have argued for thought control; Calhoun did. Ritchie said that no man, no association of men, no state or set of states had a right to withdraw from the Union on its own account, and any attempt to dissolve the Union or to obstruct the operation of the laws was treason. Calhoun said any state could exercise a veto over the Acts of Congress, and any one of them could withdraw from the Union. The early Virginians were statesmen—Calhoun and his followers were wise only in their own conceit and always wrong. They feared the end of sectionalism (the support of slavery by all Southerners). It is difficult to determine what they feared most: positive legislation by a Republican Congress to restrict slavery and to restore the high prerogatives of the Federal government, or a political revolt by the non-slaveholding whites of their own states, or a slave insurrection.

Overwhelmed at last at the ballot box despite their excessive political power, the slaveholders instituted a rebellion without justification. What did they have to offer? For the Statue of Liberty, a weeping mother leading her children to the slave market. White skins in place of habeas corpus and due process of law as guarantees of freedom. Men and women without names, branded, bred, and sold like horses in a land of free men. The whip in sharp response to prayers for justice. Millions of distressed souls consigned to living death. Mob violence in place of free inquiry and discussion. A tattered flag and a rejected Constitution. The choice of honorable men was not difficult to make.

Surrender to the demands of the slaveholders after Lincoln's election would have been an abandonment of Constitutional government, in fact of our entire Anglo-Saxon heritage in the area of government. This was a Constitutional crisis which would not admit of compromise,—concession to the slave power, perhaps, amounting to denationalization, but not compromise. Lincoln was a remarkable man. He had an abundance of common sense and unquestioned integrity. He said no compromise, knowing full well that compromise meant only concession. The only way to preserve the Union was to abolish slavery not to fortify it. The foundations of slavery were shattered by the first shots of the war. Slaveholders ran away from the advancing armies, slaves drifted into the army camps. The generals and Congress called them contrabands. They were free in any case because the exercise of force was broken. Congress abolished slavery in the District of Columbia and in the territories. The President discussed his Emancipation Proclamation, and Congress provided for complete emancipation. All of this was done almost before the armies had taken the field. A government which had been said to be subordinate to sovereign powers of the states had found new dignity and amazing strength from the courage of its young men and the vision of new leadership.

II

A NATION AND A LEGEND

A great nation was rent by war one hundred years ago; great in its wrath and great in its forgiveness. It was not easy to forgive the men who made appeal to the Gods of War and wrapped the nation in flames. It is not now easy to grasp the extent of their stupidity because only a person deeply indoctrinated in Southern mythology could believe they ever had a chance to win that war. Much about the history of the South is legendary. Relic of a mouldering past, legend disappears as man moves on into new centuries, new enlightenment, new vision. The South has been permitted to live in its past for a century, until now, out of the land of yesteryears arise mystifying stories of glories that never were.

The representatives of the slaveholding aristocracy who met at Montgomery on February 4, 1861 to establish a confederacy of slave states never succeeded. Nations are not born in such fashion, and the rebellion against Federal authority never achieved sufficient maturity, unity, or respectability to give it national status. A truly recognizable nation never emerged from the initial fury. It did not because decentralization and slavery belonged to the past and the United States government was in the hands of men who knew it. This was not a war between the states, it was a rebellion against the authority of the United States. It has to be viewed from the perspective of the Lincoln Administration, because the Davis regime was the creature of anarchy and the Lincoln Administration rested on the solid foundation of an established Constitutional government. The one was as the dying embers of a funeral pyre, the other the eternal flame of hope.

The comparison does not end there. The people had sent Lincoln to the Presidency and their men to the armies. The people, the government, the armies constituted a harmonious whole. The area, the people, the laws constituted a nation. This was not true of the Confederacy. A total of six states had sent delegates to a convention. These men, representing the slaveholding aristocracy, constituting one-third of the people, created a government, called themselves its legislative department, and chose Davis for the Presidency. Everything done thereafter was done under the shadow of military power. They printed almost worthless money, drafted men into the army, seized private property. They did not represent the people, nor enjoy the love and affection of the people. Their power was born in hate and bore a terrible harvest of hate.

The moral force of the entire Western World was arrayed against slavery. The men who organized the rebellion were in no position to obtain a place in the family of nations. Their only protection for a generation against servile insurrection and foreign interference had been the great strength of the nation. History had shown that revolutions, particularly in America, had always been accompanied by emancipation. Yet they made war to destroy the Union and its government. In doing so they destroyed slavery. History did not reverse itself. Robert Toombs opposed it bitterly, saying that the firing on Fort Sumter would be suicide. It was Toombs in the Senate a decade before who had thundered at men from the free states: "We have a right to call on you to give your blood to maintain the slaves of the South in bondage; you can not deceive others. This is a proslavery government. Slavery is stamped on its heart." And I must say parenthetically that, despite his arrogance, Toombs was correct. Slavery had reached the high noon of its existence in a subordination of Federal authority and a crippling of democratic processes. Like a hand of death it lay upon the land, reaching its ghastly fingers into the churches, the schools, the courts, and the legislative halls. The silence of the grave pervaded every species of man in the slave country because all who raised their voices against slavery fell victim to the vengeance of slaveholders. Blood flowed and in the darkness of the night it seemed that evil beyond description had fallen upon the nation.

One-hundred years have gone to join the infinity of time since those awful days, but from this distant perspective we see that the slave system alone would have dragged them down as it had the nation. Chief Justice John Marshall and Ex-President James Madison, both slaveholders, had been aware of this. Marshall had told Harriet Martineau as early as 1835 that "there was no arresting the decline of Virginia if her citizens did not put an end to slavery." Madison had said: "A society burdened with a slave system could make no permanent resistance to an unencumbered enemy; and he was astonished at the fanaticism which blinded some southern men to so clear a certainty." What agony these great statesmen must have endured had they lived to hear the ideas expressed by the intellectual pygmies who came after them.

Alexander H. Stephens, Vice-President of the Confederacy, said: "Our new goverment is founded . . . its foundations are laid, its cornerstone rests upon the great truth that the Negro is not equal to the white man; that slavery . . . is his natural and normal condition." The *Richmond Examiner* in an article, "Slavery Eternal," said: "True philanthropy to the Negro begins, like charity, at home; and if Southern men would act as if the canopy of heaven were inscribed with a covenant in letters of fire that the Negro is here and here forever, is our property and ours forever, is never to be emancipated, is to be kept hard at work and in rigid subjection all his days, and is never to go to Africa, to Polynesia, or to Yankee land, they would accomplish more good for the race in five years than they boast the institution to have accomplished in two centuries." Men in the heart of the Black Belt today are not deceived about the purpose of the rebellion one hundred years ago even if historians would like to minimize it. All discussion of emancipation was summarily suppressed in the South until near the end of the war. General Patrick Cleburne, finding soldiers unwilling to re-enlist after Missionary Ridge, drew up proposals to free the slaves and bring them into the Army. Thirteen of General Joseph E. Johnston's staff signed these proposals but Johnston and President Davis suppressed them and serious discussion by the Secretary of War and others followed of the unpleasant aspects of a policy of extermination, as if it were more desirable than emancipation. When slaves started running away by the thousands, and were abandoned by stampeding masters, it was apparent that the basis for rebellion was greatly weakened and the power of the aristocracy was gone. Unable to establish their own independence, they debated putting muskets into the hands of the slaves and imploring them to fight for the permanent slavery of themselves. That was their policy at the end.

Rebellion was not a remedy for the South's fancied grievances. It did not provide security. It did not provide strength. Calhoun had so hypnotized the Southern people that they had lost their reason. They never regained it. Decentralization and local autonomy were well designed to break up a nation but they were ill-suited to the task of building one. Decentralization was contrary to the needs of developing industrialism and to conducting a war. There was dissension in the slave states from the first over secession. The states of the upper South were bitter about having to choose between being a helpless minority in the United States or joining the Confederacy after all important decisions had been made. Four of these slave states remained loyal and furnished more men to the Union than to the Confederate armies. The Appalachian Highland was intensely loyal to the Union. Every state except South Carolina had a strong Unionist minority. Tennessee had left the Union only after the governor entered into a treasonable military alliance and the state was overrun by a Confederate army. Tremendous pressure was put upon the convention of Virginia by armed Knights of the Golden Circle to take the state out of the Union, and following secession the Western third of the state formed its own loyal government. Tennessee gave the United States a war-time Vice-President. The great General George H. Thomas was a Virginian by birth, and the indomitable Admiral Farragut was born in Tennessee. The Ozark region was strongly opposed to the war, and in Sam Houston's Texas one-third of the people were neutral and one-third Unionist.

Men walked blindly into this strange adventure or were dragooned into it in various ways as the 18,000 petitions for pardons, with supporting documents, zealously kept from the prying eyes of historians for generations, so admirably show. They were soon alienated from each other. There came a day when Henry S. Foote of Tennessee said of Davis in the Confederate Congress: "Others may vote to extend this man's power for mischief; I hold in contempt him and his whole tribe of servitors and minions." He subsequently resigned from the Congress and left the Confederacy after a short term in prison. Robert Toombs, made Secretary of State, proved unfit for both civil and military duty, first resigning from the Cabinet post and then from the Army after challenging General D. H. Hill to a duel.

Toombs' colleague from Georgia, Alexander H. Stephens, had been one of the architects of the Kansas-Nebraska Act and a strong champion of slavery and renewal of the African trade. He was opposed to secession, did not believe in the Confederacy, and in his heart never left the Union. He was denounced by many of the aristocrats as a poor man turned demagogue, and probably was denied an opportunity for the Presidency through fear that he would negotiate immediately for reunion. Had the full extent of his personal feelings been known, he might well have been killed at Montgomery for he had no faith in the movement or its leaders. He was chosen Vice-President, remained away from Richmond for a year and a half and aided and abetted Governor Joseph E. Brown of Georgia in opposition to the Conscription Acts. William L. Yancey, without whose impassioned oratory secession might never have reached unmanageable proportions, failed in his mission to secure British aid, returned to join the opposition in the Confederate Congress, and died a sadly disillusioned man. What he may have said about it all must remain a mystery because his papers were destroyed by fire.

The Appalachian Highland not only sent thousands of men into the Union armies, its leaders were closely akin to the views of Stephens. Governors Joseph E. Brown of Georgia and Zebulon B. Vance of North Carolina openly challenged the authority of President Davis and his Congress. The mountain area was a part of the Confederate States of America only because it was a part of states officially belonging to the Confederacy. It gave no allegiance to the Confederate government but was under the authority of state governments and greatly influenced those governments. It was non-slaveholding, self-sufficient, strongly Unionist. It had opposed secession, and favored restoration of normal relationships in the Union. The Confederacy resorted to conscription almost at once and these people resorted to resistance. The same was true of every non-slaveholding section of the seceding states. Men were deserting from the army by thousands as Grant and Sherman moved south in 1862. Desertions increased as the war continued, greatly hampering Lee in his operations. He left the Rapidan in 1863 with 85,000 men, lost 28,000 at Gettysburg, and recrossed the Potomac with only 35,000. So many surrendered at the end of Pickett's charge that approaching Union artillery units thought Seminary Ridge had been captured. Two-thirds of Hood's army deserted in 1864. Many of the known 103,000 deserters became guerrilas; many went north and joined the Union armies; many deserted and went about as they pleased in the Southern cities. Thousands surrendered and refused to be exchanged, preferring to take an oath of allegiance and go free. In some cases they totaled one-fourth of those in a prison camp. Governor Shorter of Alabama requested that two companies of Alabamans serving in the Union army and captured by Nathan Bedford Forrest's Rangers be turned over to his state to be tried for treason. Prowling bands of cavalry had complete control of Northern Georgia for twelve months before the end of the war. A peace society, with secret rituals, flourished in Arkansas, Mississippi, Alabama, Georgia, and Tennessee; and, if we can trust the records of the United States Court of Claims, 22,298 persons furnished $60,000,000 worth of supplies to the Union armies.

Nearly 30,000 able-bodied men were kept from military service by appointments from Governors Brown and Vance to state offices. Brown had been a mighty force for secession, Vance a strong Unionist. They belonged, in reality, neither to the Confederacy nor to the Union. They were devotees of state rights. Here was a classic example of the fact that although state rights might destroy the Union, it would never create a Confederacy. State rights to these men, as to Stephens, was not a matter of convenience, it was a faith. Conscription by the Davis regime was a direct and complete death blow to the theory and practice of state sovereignty. These men would have none of it. They insisted upon nullifying acts of the Confederate Congress, and unable to convince their legislatures to do so, resorted to exemptions and appointments to office. The governors of Alabama, Mississippi, and Texas followed, leaving the Davis government little support in its efforts to maintain an army.

Economically the Confederacy had no basis for its existence. Southern newspapers had freely predicted the ruin of the nation's banks, railroads, and factories. Loss of Southern trade was to bring poverty to Northern wage earners and mob violence in industrial centers. Southern leaders sneered at the possibility of a blockade, but the day came when any device was welcomed to secure an ounce of quinine or calomel, when persimmon seeds were used for buttons and sweet potatoes were used for coffee. Trade between the slave states and the North was said to have enriched the North alone, but cut off from that trade the South was impoverished. The world's economy was said to be so seriously dependent upon raw cotton that aid to the cause of the Confederacy was certain but Europe did not intervene.

The entire economy of the rebellious area collapsed during the war. In fact Confederate soldiers were frequently barefoot before the battle of Shiloh, and they were so undernourished that the death rate among prisoners was exceedingly high during the first weeks of internment. The army was hungry before the autumn of 1861. Unable to find food, it followed the practice of seizing everything within an operational radius of its camps and entire populations of civilians were forced by near starvation to abandon their communities and move. Three and one-half billion dollars in paper currency was issued on a basis of 27 million dollars in gold and silver. This money was worth only eight cents on the dollar after Gettysburg and Vicksburg (July,

1863). Eggs sold for $6.00 per dozen, butter for $25.00 per pound, shoes for $125.00 per pair, and flour for $275.00 per barrel at a time when soldiers were paid $11.00 per month. The cavalry steadily deteriorated for lack of horseshoes. Railroad transportation broke down completely because there were no replacements for rails and rolling stock.

The lot of the people in the relatively small area of rebellion went from poverty to privation. The government collected taxes in kind. Farmers lost their horses, mules, and wagons. They were very reluctant to raise foodstuffs, or to sell to agents of the government either for currency or promises to pay. They hid their livestock and harvested grain and sent as much produce into commercial channels as possible. They were afraid to venture upon the roads with their horses and wagons. Cavalry and wagon trains fed upon the cornfields and officers gave the farmers receipts which were rejected by the tax collectors. There were bread riots in Richmond, Mobile, and Salisbury, North Carolina; and pilfering made the task of moving army supplies through the cities almost impossible. Worse still imposters seized property and left worthless receipts. Finally thousands of farmers stopped trying to raise anything. The Davis government confiscated as much as it could and passed out of existence owing 500 millions of dollars to the impoverished farmers. Less than ten per cent of the industries and skilled labor of the United States was in these states. There were only six million people in the whole of the rebellious area, not more than one-half of them in what remained after Vicksburg fell. Only nine thousand of the thirty thousand miles of railroad were in the area and little of it could be maintained. Trains were forced to reduce speeds to ten miles per hour by early 1863. All of the railroads ceased to operate by the end of the war. Open revolt was close to a reality by the summer of 1864. Most significant of all, aid to soldiers' families by people in many communities ceased as despair of success increased. Even where there was food, there was no faith.

We say that Lincoln was President of the United States and Jefferson Davis was President of the Confederate States of America. This is true only in name, not in reality. On the one hand we had a nation, a rapidly growing, prosperous nation; a nation of vast extent, reaching from the Atlantic to the Pacific; a nation with an agricultural empire of homestead farmers and a rapidly expanding industrial empire. There were a million veterans in the nation's armies in 1865, and more men available for military service than there had been in 1861. The Confederacy had none of this expanse, mineral resources, agriculture, or industry, or foreign trade, and little man-power. The pitiful remnants of Lee's and Johnston's armies were in rags and starving at the end. There was deep unrest in the area of rebellion from the very beginning. Some of it came from a distrust of Davis who was an irascible man, somewhat of a dictator. Some of it came from a long existing hostility toward the slaveholding aristocracy. Some of it was pure state rights philosophy of the Alexander Stephens brand. Some of it came from an awakening realization that the war was hastening emancipation. Some of it came from the complete failure of Davis to control the economy. Much of it came from the loss of life in a cause without sign of benefit.

Given, then, infirmity of purpose on the part of the government, downright opposition by a large portion of the people, and a crumbling economy, from whence came spiritual sustenance for the army and to what end were their sacrifices made? There is only one answer: sectionalism as we have defined it, patriotism as a Southerner of 1860 would have called it, the central theme of Southern history as Phillips so cogently described it. It was unswerving devotion, not to the nation but to the deviating mores of a geographical area within the nation—devotion to the point of uncritical and unreasoning support of its institutions and its laws however harmful they might be to the nation's unity, prestige, and high prerogatives in relation to other nations and its own citizens. It meant that, as a price of union and peace, the nation must remain a white man's nation in which people of color should never aspire to equality of rights or to a voice in political affairs. They must remain an inferior people even if free and their control must remain decentralized. Search as one will, this was the one thing common to most Southerners and to them alone. They could keep it only by a maximum of decentralization. This belief in inferiority of people of color and in their own superiority was combined in their Congressional speeches before the war, in the pleas of secession leaders, in the communiques of field commanders to their men, and in the speeches of governors, even of President Davis. Soldiers of the nation to which they owed everything were Yankee invaders, "Hessians from the North, hirelings, mercenary cowards," as Governor Rector of Arkansas called them, a mean, selfish, vulgar people who wished to free the slaves and make them equals of the white people.

So it was that the Confederate soldier, in spite of false hopes, erroneous conjectures, incompetent leadership; in spite of unreasonable demands, insufficient food and clothing, fought to the bitter end. His valor gave his people unity in defeat, something the people, especially the women, could talk about and linger over for generations to come: a flag, a tradition, an inheritance of Southernism which is very real but can neither be described nor defined, because it is so irrational. General D. H. Hill came about as close to it as anyone when he wrote to General Foster of the Union army in 1863: "It is no business of yours if we chose to burn one of our own towns. A meddling Yankee troubles himself about everybody's matters except his own and repents of everybody's sins except his own. We are different people. ... No one knows better than yourself that there is not a respectable man in North Carolina in any condition of life who is not utterly and irrevocably opposed to union with your hated and hateful people."

The Lincoln Administration whose elevation to

power had been the occasion for rebellion was the first in the nation's history to face up to the question of human rights versus slavery. It was to be the last to do so for another hundred years. The Republican party was a new party come to power. It was basically an antislavery party dating back to 1840. Political action against slavery had been necessary for a number of reasons. State laws discriminating against people of color had to be repealed. The majesty of the law, dethroned by mobs and obsequious politicians, had to be restored. The supremacy of the Federal government had to be re-asserted and acknowledged. Congress and the Courts had to be rescued from domination by an oligarchy of slaveholders. Something had to be done to protect people against kidnapping by marauding slaveholders and their agents. The seat of government had to be made accessible to all citizens. The right of all citizens to move about freely had to be acknowledged. Slavery had to be cleared out of the territories. The sale of human beings had to stop. Slavery had to be put in course of ultimate extinction.

All of these things had to be done by political action but no political party to which slaveholders belonged would do them. Political action was necessary because the slave states simply refused to discuss the subject. An independent political party was necessary because slaveholders controlled both of the existing parties. Antislavery men had to consolidate their political power. They did this in 1839-40, organizing the Liberty party on a single principle of opposition to slavery and nominating a former slaveholder, James G. Birney, one of the greatest antislavery leaders, for the Presidency.

This memorable action was taken by a mere handful of courageous men in New York state. It gave men like James G. Birney, Henry B. Stanton, Alvan Stewart, Myron Holley, and Gerrit Smith a high place in the political history of the nation. It gave the United States its one chance of survival with Constitutional government. These men were determined to abolish slavery within the framework of the Union, to restore the supremacy of Federal authority, and to preserve the Union. They reorganized as the Free Soil party in 1848 and again as the Republican party in 1854. They won the Presidential Election of 1860. Southern politicians had claimed sovereignty for the states and had succeeded to a degree in subordinating Federal authority to that of the states. They had translated the decentralizing philosophy of Jefferson into the state rights philosophy of Calhoun and Yancey. They had demanded new political machinery giving them local autonomy, and being refused, had resorted to the fiction of state secession and a separate government in defense of slavery.

Antislavery men held the natural rights of man to be superior to man-made law. They reverenced the basic documents which recognized these rights, our numerous institutions which safeguarded and protected these rights, and the government to the degree that it performed its several duties in harmony with these rights. They were adamant in insisting that the Constitution be interpreted in accordance with the principles stated in the Declar-tion of Independense and intended to have a Supreme Court which would so interpret.

The antislavery men were all Republicans but not in complete agreement by any means. Some men held that the courts must free the slaves in any cases brought before them on the ground that slavery was abolished by the Declaration of Independence; that no state had a republican form of government, as guaranteed by the Constitution, if its laws recognized enslavement by force of one portion of its people by another portion; that the Constitution did not use the word slave but the word person, and persons could not be property; that slaves had not been deprived of liberty by due process of law.

A far greater number of antislavery men held, variously, that slavery was an exercise of force, recognized by state law, the status of the slave changing to that of a free man when the exercise of force ceased through flight of the slave or of the slaveholder or withdrawal of support by the state; that any slave who came into or was brought into a free state, or escaped to the high seas was automatically free, slavery having no constitutional status; that the Fugitive Slave Act was unconstitutional, among other reasons, because it flagrantly violated due process of law; that color as a presumption of slavery was impossible to apply and a threat to the freedom of all persons; that people of color were citizens of the United States, parties to the Constitution, and entitled to all the privileges and immunities of citizens. Practically all antislavery men held that Congress had power under the Constitution to abolish slavery in the District of Columbia and in the territories; to abolish the interstate slave trade; and to refuse admission to new slave states. They agreed that Congress should repeal the Fugitive Slave Act.

Beyond all of these possible lines of action was general emancipation, and that was something else entirely. There had been three possibilities: purchase of the slaves, perhaps with proceeds from the public lands; emancipation by amendment of the Federal Constitution; and emancipation under the war powers. Some day historians may get around to admitting that slavery was abolished when the first shots were fired at Fort Sumter. Every shot fired thereafter removed the chains from another slave. Once the rebellion had been suppressed, however long it might have taken, and however much the cost, slavery would have been so disorganized that nothing short of the full power of the Federal government could ever have restored it. The main problem was putting down the rebellion, on which there was more than adequate support for the Lincoln Administration though not unanimity in the country.

The second problem which faced Lincoln was in the area of international relations. There may have been times when our government could have afforded to disregard world opinion, but not when it was faced with a formidable rebellion against its authority, and neither then nor now on the question of human relations. The United States was the land of slavery. Slavery was peculiarly an American institution. The Confederacy rested its case at home on the defense of slavery but carefully nurtured the idea abroad that slavery had nothing to do with the war. Historians have fallen into the trap. Why should not Europe have done so? Because Lincoln, Seward, and Sumner, the three men wholly responsible, found and sent to Europe, the Far East, Russia, Canada, and Mexico strong antislavery men who could be depended upon to correct the wrong impression of the nation's ideals and objectives in the war. This was something diplomats had to do, Lincoln having to emphasize at home that objective —preservation of the Union—which had the strongest and widest appeal and which, once accomplished, automatically served the additional purpose of abolishing slavery.

They sought cultivated men who spoke the language of freedom. They were men who had insisted for thirty years that freedom throughout the world would never be secure until the government of the United States was placed on the side of freedom and the country returned to the ancient faith of the Declaration. James S. Pike of the *New York Tribune,* where the flag was lowered to half-mast after the Missouri Valley was opened to slavery, had said: "You can not compromise a question of human freedom for its relations and influences go beyond the stars, and its bearing and connections are eternal." George G. Fogg of the *Independent Democrat* had written: "It is not the fate of Kansas only that is at stake. It is the fate of the continent and it may be of humanity the world over and in all coming time." Anson Burlingame had declared of the Fugitive Slave Act: "We shall no more remain quiet until it is repealed than we would at midnight with a rattlesnake in our beds." Zebina Eastman had prophesied that if we did not put an end to slavery "The people that are to live on this soil for a thousand generations to come, whether they be white or black, will rise up to curse the people of this generation—and God will certainly damn it with a fiery damnation." John Bigelow of the New York *Evening Post* solemnly proclaimed that "four more years of pro-slavery administration would have been almost more than our Constitution could have withstood." William Dean Howells had written to his father: "If I were not your son, I would desire to be Old John Brown's. God bless him!" "The unprofitableness of slavery is a monstrous evil," said Hinton Rowan Helper, "it makes us poor; poverty makes us wretched; wretchedness makes us wicked; and wickedness leads to the devil." There were many others of great stature, including the historian John Lothrop Motley, the veteran statesman Thomas Corwin, and Joshua Giddings, stalwart leader in the battles against the Gag Resolution, the Fugitive Slave Act, and the Mexican War. These were the Thomas Paines, the Benjamin Franklins, and the Anthony Benezets of the 1860's.

Given success by his armies and diplomats, the road ahead for Lincoln was straight and clear but not so easily traversed. Slavery was one thing, the belief in biological inferiority was something else again. Slavery was complete subjection of one person to the will of another, but it was also control and subordination of all slaves by the white population. The first was an individual relationship, the second a system with far-reaching ramifications. The institution of slavery enshrined the doctrine of racialism. Abolishing the personal relationship would not necessarily abolish the doctrine of racial inequality, nor abolish slavery as a system. Most people were thinking of slavery in the narrow sense. Certainly colonizationists were, and the anti-war Democrats. This was the reason antislavery people had never looked with favor upon purchase, Constitutional Amendment, or war, because none of these methods would deal with the problem of individual accountability, repentance or retributive justice. Freedom for the slaves was greatly to be desired, however it could be accomplished, but freedom would be robbed of its luster if the white people remained devotees of racial ideology, refused to give to the people of color free status as citizens, and denied them their natural rights. It would be an incomplete freedom.

Antislavery people for whom Senator Charles Sumner and Representative Thaddeus Stevens were spokesmen in Congress believed in a policy of immediate and complete emancipation. Free persons of color, among whom there were many brilliant, cultivated, and highly respected citizens of the free states, fugitives escaping in increasing numbers, and even slaves to the degree that they understood the issue, took the same positon. Four hundred years of agonizing struggle to regain their freedom and recognition as persons were now behind these people. Antislavery people had been battling for more than a generation to free the slaves and protect democratic institutions. This was the day of atonement, of the final contest between human rights and slavery for control of the nation. Here was a conflict of armies and of ideas; a struggle to preserve Constitutional government, and to establish for all time equality of all persons; a battle to the death between a firmly established, constitutionally organized government and a powerful composite of dissent.

The people of color were in the middle of this ideological and military turmoil. They had to make decisions. They were of many minds, as were the white people. They spoke out, sometimes with bitterness and impatience but with amazing unanimity in support of sound principles. They spoke as members of a democratic society under a government of law and in a language which free men understood, yet they themselves were not wholly free. Some people still shouted at them in ways more powerful than words that they were not men. They had been doing so for 300 years. Some states denied them the right to participate in political affairs, and subjected them to laws they did not help to make. They could not always move about as they pleased. They did not enjoy equal economic opportunity and educational advantages. They did not always get impartial treatment at the hands of law enforcement officials, but the consummation of this long struggle for freedom and equality was near. The destiny of the nation and their own destiny were being fused in the flames of war.

Here, as in everything else pertaining to the Civil War, we have to come back to Lincoln and his armies for proper perspective. There was an initial reluctance on the part of the government to enroll persons of color in the armed services despite ample precedent for doing so. There could have been many reasons: fear of a general racial war, opposition of a large segment of civilians and soldiers loyally supporting the government, or even the logical position that white men must pay the price of their folly and not ask the people of color, who had been wronged so grievously, to bear this further burden. But the people of color were not to be denied. Until they wore the uniform of a soldier, had a rifle in their hands, and stood shoulder to shoulder with other citizens in defense of the government they had no certain claim to equality of rights.

The drama which unfolded about free people of color, fugitives, and slaves would require many volumes in the telling. Armies had not yet taken the field, in fact armies of respectable size had not yet been organized, when generals were plagued by the problem of fugitive slaves. There was a brief period in which some field commanders, left to their own resources, would not permit fugitives to come within their lines, even surrendered them to claimants. General Benjamin Butler, May 24, 1861, in Virginia, called them contrabands, and 'contrabands' they were in common parlance thereafter, despite the fact they were not property, nor was the Confederacy out of the Union. Butler refused to surrender them to anyone and demanded to know of the War Department the status of women and children not used by the enemy on war projects. Some generals, acting at their own discretion, of whom McClellan is the outstanding example, sought to infringe upon the powers of civil government by insisting that slavery should remain undisturbed by the war. Other generals, John C. Fremont in Missouri (July 30, 1861) and David Hunter in South Carolina and Georgia (April 11, 1862) issued emancipation pronouncements in their respective areas of operations and properly so under the rules of war, but they were disallowed by Lincoln who reserved to himself the exercise of such powers.

Congress, whose session had not begun until July 1, followed Butler's lead and passed, August 6, 1861, the First Confiscation Act making subject to seizure all property (slaves) used in the rebellion. Winter came, Forts Donelson and Henry were captured but Shiloh was a month away and McClellan had not yet moved on the Peninsula, when Lincoln proposed financial aid for emancipation and Congress forbade return of fugitive slaves by the military forces. Ten days after Shiloh, April 16, slavery was abolished in the District of Columbia, with a provision for compensation not to exceed $300 to the owner and voluntary colonization to Haiti or Liberia. The colonization provision was repealed in 1864. Congress provided by Treaty, May 20, for full cooperation with Great Britain in suppressing the African slave trade, abolished slavery in all of the territories without compensation to the owners on June 19, and passed the Second Confiscation Act, July 17, providing freedom for the slaves of all persons aiding in the rebellion. Four days before this final action by Congress, Lincoln had informed Secretaries Seward and Welles that he was considering a proclamation of general emancipation. He read one to his Cabinet July 23, issued his Preliminary Proclamation after the victory at Antietam, September 17, 1862, and his final Proclamation on January 1, 1863.

This brought the issue back to the army, for the action by Congress and the President constituted nothing more, really, than a definition of policy. The slaves were as free as they had been able to make themselves with the aid of the army and as free as they were going to be without further military aid. That is about the way the matter stood until the Constitution was amended. The Thirteenth Amendment was introduced in Congress March 25, 1864, was finally passed January 31, 1865, and was proclaimed a part of the Constitution December 18, 1865. It was with good reason the free people of color looked to the Army rather than to Congress, and to Lincoln as Commander-in-Chief rather than as Chief Executive. The incompetence of Congress to deal with the problem had already begun and was to continue for a hundred years.

The story of the army and people of color is one

of the most fascinating in the nation's history. Wherever the armies went in the South the slaves gave them guidance, aid, and comfort. They never betrayed a Union soldier. The slave system was completely disorganized from the beginning. Sherman found the Confederacy an empty shell. He could go wherever he pleased, and he sent a detachment of troops over to destroy Meridian, Mississippi. It came back followed by 8000 slaves strung out for ten miles along the road, some of whom had come for 300 miles. While marching north from Savannah he had to detach troops to escort 5,000 to New Berne and 10,000 to Wilmington. At times the armies were bogged down by an avalanche of fugitives. These people brought to the army valuable information of every sort. They served as spies, as guides, as laborers, and eventually as soldiers.

The army, sparing time from its military objectives, accepted them into the warmth and security of the camps. The generals put them to work, then organized schools for them. The benevolent societies contributed more than one million dollars and hundreds of teachers. The officers and men taught them in the refugee camps. The government established a commission to study the program and out of it came systematic education in refugee camps, occupied towns and abandoned plantations. A public school system was established during the war without money by the combined efforts of the army and antislavery people.

Most important of all, however, was the teaching

of the soldiers by fellow white officers and men on a man to man basis. Lincoln's Emancipation Proclamation instructed the armed services to aid and assist fugitives in every possible way, something they had been doing for a long time, and to enroll them into the army. Well trained units were ready to serve, and eventually 186,000 men, including many fugitives wrote a brilliant record of service to their country, paving the way to a constitutional guarantee of citizenship and equality. There are those who still believe and say we gave the slaves their freedom.

Let no man say we gave what God had first
bestowed.
Virtue does not shine so bright in restoration;
Nor does redemption come by way of sacrifice
Of slaves and freeborn boys who found on battle-
fields
The dignity of man, the unity of peoples.
Set free from chains on limbs and eyes that could
not see,
Death seemed to be their only road to truth at last.
The land was cursed by long sustained injustice.
The souls of men were warped by sin and suffering
Beyond redemption.
These men died with courage, then lay in unmarked
graves,
While traitors lived in honor, luxury and ease,
Compelled subordination of the freed-man
By ignorance, poverty, heavy hand of death,
Mobs, guns, whips, fire, obsequious politicians.

A nation saved from treason, rebels back in power!
Heroes dead, largely forgotten, black men
reenslaved!
A powerful nation, smug in its self conceit,
Saved by its slaves, now scorned in their own
homeland.
Saved for what!
A restless nation, filled with hate, disquietude.
Restless as the boys in blue, asleep in patriots
graves.
Restless because it turned aside from destiny.
Men knew the promise of their sires to recognize
Equality and dignity of all people;
That justice called for wholesale retribution;
Yet, would not give in life what others gave by
death;
Preferring not to lead or even keep abreast
Of man's eternal quest for peace and happiness
In other lands.

III

DRUMMER BOY TO GENERAL

When one speaks of warfare, what does one talk
about?
Unknown dead, empty chairs, widows who weep
alone,
Men who leave their smithies, factories, farms, and
shops,
Death which lurks in every forest, ditch and fence
row,
The graves of those who died, which mark the battle-
field,
Murderous bushwhackers who wore no uniforms
And tried to pass as peaceful men when come upon,
Desertions, courts martial, spies, enemy agents,
Bayonets, minnie balls, sabers, shrapnel, rifles,
All instruments of death.

Crashing martial music, tramp of marching soldiers,
Inspired melodies, cocked hats, gay uniforms,
Officers, conceited and hated, or beloved,
Mud and mules, wagon trains, railroads, pontoon
bridges,
Dirty drinking water, typhoid fever, scurvy,
Heroes and deserters, poker players and saints,
Camp followers, sutlers, drummer boys, paymasters,
Volunteers and draftees, bounties and substitutes,
Hospitals and campfires, marching, drilling, waiting,
Waiting for peace.

There is no end to life's complexities; there was none for the men at war. Death did not hunt for them, they went to seek it out, bearing love of home and country, hoping to live for one, prepared to die for the other, and from that search came a consciousness of new strength in the nation.

The nation responded to Lincoln's call to arms with vast and untiring energy. It had manpower. It had industry, transportation, riches. It had a far-flung, expanding, agricultural empire of homestead farms. It was building a vast new railroad system, a new banking system, and iron and oil industries. The vibrant energies of its people knew no restraints. Suddenly they were faced by the harshest baptism of fire any people had ever endured. There was a rebellion against the authority of the United States government. The fountainhead or directive agency of rebellion, called the Davis government, sought out the most secure place in the slave states and sat there throughout its short life protected by the defense line of its best general and by the mountains.

Normal economic life in the disaffected areas of the country was at a standstill for four years. Southern economy had revolved about cotton and cotton production ceased. The war was an annoyance to the rest of the United States. The North and West were bursting out all over with schemes for economic progress. They went on about their business during the war, building railroads to the Pacific, admitting new states, developing a great wheat empire, expanding iron mining, manufacturing and commerce on the Great Lakes, developing a new national banking system. Putting down the rebellion was a distasteful job that had to be done. They sent their young men off to do it and went on about their business.

There were less than 25,000 men in the army when Fort Sumter was fired upon, almost none of them available for defense of Washington. Lincoln's request, April 15, 1861, for 75,000 state militia for three months brought nearly 100,000 men into the army and it was these men who bought precious time at Bull Run. Six hundred forty thousand volunteers were in the service by December. A half-million more were turned away for lack of equipment. Within a year these volunteers from farm and factory were welded into an army that surpassed Europe's finest. They fought the great battles of the spring and summer of 1862. A request for 300,000 more in July 1862 brought in 421,000 for three years; and it was these three-year volunteers of 1862 together with 136,000 veterans who re-enlisted in 1863 for the duration of the war, who finished it and to whom this nation owes its greatest debt. These men were not mercenaries nor draftees. They did not fight for the paltry $15.00 per month allowance. They had families at home and they returned easily and quickly to peace-time pursuits at the end of the war.

The people wanted these boys well used and they wanted victory as quickly and cheaply in terms of lives as possible. Lincoln had to provide their field commanders. The reputations of these generals depended upon the men. They sorted out the generals in their own collective mind pretty fast, more rapidly than Lincoln could because politics, seniority and distorted reports were a great encumbrance to him. More rapidly and more convincingly but not as cheaply because one incompetent general and one battle added up to thousands of dead and made a mockery of courage. The soldiers fought their own war for the most part. Lincoln had to keep trying and eventually found his men.

What did Lincoln and his soldiers want? Generals who were concerned about the food, health, and general comfort of their men. Generals who were fully conscious of the quality of their men, capable of committing them to battle intelligently, and willing to drive forward to the limit of their capacity. Generals who kept to their own area of competence and responsibility, recognizing the superior authority of the civil government and leaving to others the determination of public policy. Generals who fought and fought again until they were told to stop. In short, generals who would create the army into an instrument of the highest perfection and use it as befit a machine whose parts were the best of a nation's manhood. Generals who would blend into the pattern of ideals, objectives, and dedication expressed by the deeds of the army and the words of their Commander-in-Chief.

The job that Lincoln's armies had to do took them along roads from Bull Run to Appomattox and from Shiloh to Raleigh, and branching out from these roads along divers bypaths leading to rebel strongholds. The first of these roads was less than a hundred miles long; the second was not far as the crow flies but it swung south around the ranges of mountains that protected the heart of the Confederacy. Along these roads armies surged forward and receded, and always the Union armies moved a little nearer their ultimate goal of restoring the authority of the government over territory from which it had been dislodged.

Far off to the West the rebel dreams of empire were systematically shattered: Fort Donelson (February 16, 1862), Island No. 10 (March 14), Shiloh (April 6-7), New Orleans (April 29), Corinth (October 3), Vicksburg (July 4, 1863). The route from the great interior to South America and Africa as Lincoln had described it was open. Whatever flimsy hopes ever existed of dragooning the upper Mississippi Valley into disunion were gone. The West, territories and states alike, was cut away from the source of disaffection and the Davis regime from whatever material resources and manpower it had in that region. The nation also had found its generals in this short space of time—Grant and Sherman, McPherson and Thomas, Sheridan and the indomitable Admiral Farragut—and had built for Lincoln a fresh water navy.

Farther east, Lincoln had worried about the loyal people of the mountains, in Tennessee particularly, and the need to rescue them from their oppressions, to reestablish civil government in the area, and to get on with the business of emancipation, but the Army of the Cumberland was commanded by Buell and then by Rosecrans. Buell did not believe in the war's objectives and Rosecrans wanted to keep banker's hours. He dilly-dallied and temporized, won a battle at Stone's River, forced his opponent back to Chickamauga, and there by the River of Death would have lost an army but for Thomas and Sheridan. A few weeks later (September 23-24, 1863), three veteran armies of Sherman, Thomas and Hooker (sent from the East) drove Bragg's army in hopeless confusion off Missionary Ridge and Lookout Mountain and back into Georgia. Sherman still had to get around the mountains and to him fell the task of defeating the second best general of the Confederacy: Joseph E. Johnston.

What then of Virginia? There was Lee protecting his government at Richmond—to what purpose? His state for which he had left the Union and violated his oath of allegiance was being devastated. His new government was far more dictatorial than his former one had been. Only twice did he leave the state, venturing across the Potomac where thousands of his soldiers would not follow him in daredevil gambles without purpose and without hope; driven back each time with terrific losses; refusing to leave his state for the West; drawing more and more as the war progressed upon the coastal defenses for replacements. There was, therefore, a constant constriction of the rebellious area as Union armies moved south and inland from the coast. There in Northern Virginia along the Rappahannock and on the Peninsula, month after weary month, men from the Southland, conscripted from the early days of the war and funneled into Lee's army, defended a military frontier to no purpose because the war was being lost in the West, and there was nothing Lee or his men or his corps commanders could do in Virginia to prevent the inevitable collapse of armed resistance to the Lincoln government.

There were about 2,778,000 men in the Union armies at one time or another. The Confederates had 1,300,000. Reducing these figures to three-year enlistments, we have 1,500,000 and 1,000,000, with lives lost 359,000 and 258,000. More than two million of the men in the Union armies were less than twenty-two years of age and 1,151,000 under nineteen at the time of enlistment. Army regulations specified 18 to 45, but more than 200,000 were less than eighteen and one of George H. Thomas' drummer boys from Michigan was nine years of age. The Union army was an army of young men. Philip Sheridan was 30, James B. McPherson 33, George B. McClellan 35, W. S. Hancock 37, U. S. Grant 39, and W. T. Sherman 41. The soldiers were so young they called these men old. Confederate soldiers were both younger and older because the Davis government started conscripting men from 18 to 35 in April, 1862, raised the age limit to 45 in September, and changed the ages to 17 and 50 in February, 1864. Lee and Joseph E. Johnston were 54, and Albert Sidney Johnston was 58, but the brilliant corps commanders were younger men. Stonewall Jackson was only 35, A. P. Hill 36, James Longstreet 40, and "Jeb" Stuart 28.

The Union army was a volunteer army. In fact almost everything about the war was done on a voluntary basis from serving in the army to financing the government through purchase of government bonds. There were not more than 10,000 drafted men in the Union army before the summer of 1863, and not very many among the 1,000,000 veteran troops when Lee and Johnston surrendered the tattered remnants of their armies in April, 1865. Getting drafted men anywhere and keeping them was like handling quicksilver. Lincoln said getting them from Washington to the Army of the Potomac was like shoveling fleas across a barnyard. There was a bounty system which brought a host of undesirables into the service. There was a system by which men of means could hire substitutes if they were drafted. Fifty thousand men paid $300 each to buy exemptions. There were bounty jumpers who enlisted, deserted, and enlisted again. The real source of inefficiency, however, was higher.

In the war department a very bad practice was followed of forming new regiments instead of sending replacements to veteran units; a system doubly pernicious because governors were allowed to appoint regimental officers and the army was always cluttered with political appointees to the end result of unnecessary losses and impaired morale. There was criminal neglect in the training of competent officers. There were officers of high rank who refused to serve under men of lesser rank, and there were some who left the service because of personal pique. Despite all of this, the men who did everything wrong at Bull Run, did everything right at Gettysburg. Soldiers fought and won battles when the generals did not know where their own armies were, much less the enemy. They proved that lack of roads and railroads, and that mud and water, climate and disease were not insuperable obstacles. In the end, the armies which Grant and Sherman led through Washington were the most splendid fighting machines the world had ever seen. General Joseph E. Johnston said there had not been an army like Sherman's since the days of Julius Caesar.

The basic unit of the army was a regiment. A Union soldier always spoke of his regiment as an ordinary civilian speaks of his town or city, or if from Virginia or Ohio, of his county. The histories of the war are regimental histories. There are more than five hundred of them. Four or five regiments constituted a brigade under a brigadier-general. The average infantry regiment had about one thousand men but its average effective strength was about seven hundred. There were slightly more than two thousand regiments in the Union army, each commanded by a colonel who was the key to successful training and distinguished service. There were two or more battalions to a regiment, each commanded by a major, and eight companies to a battalion, each commanded by a captain. Men were very proud of their regiments, and some of them became famous: Forty-eighth New York (Perry's Saints); Thirty-third Illinois (Teachers) reputed to have disregarded commands not given in proper syntax or orthography; One Hundredth Indiana (Persimmon Regiment); Thirty-seventh Iowa (Greybeard Regiment) all 45 years or older, three-fourths with long white beards; Forty-fourth New York, all under 30, unmarried, at least 5 ft. 8 in., good moral character; Berdans' Sharpshooters of which each recruit had to be able to fire ten shots at a distance of 600 feet within five inches of a bull's eye, and all ten shots in the bull's eye at 300 feet. Regiments had pets and mascots ranging all the way from bald eagles to brown bears.

Since people of distinct national origin have always lived in compact settlements, urban and rural, and companies were formed on a local basis, regiments sometimes were definitely Swedish, German, Irish, French, and so forth. There developed a legend in the slave states that mercenary troops were recruited abroad to subdue the American South. Actually, 82 per cent of the men in the volunteer army were born in the United States and more than 90 per cent were citizens. Only 175,000 had been born in Germany, 150,000 in Ireland, 50,000 in England, and 100,000 in other countries—less than the normal percentage of foreign born in our population at any time before the first world war. Nor was this a war of New England upon the South. The Old Southwest—Alabama, Mississippi, and Louisiana—provided the initiative and the leadership in trying to break up the Union, and the Old Northwest responded better than the East to the call for troops. Only 17 percent of the volunteers came from New England, and 80 per cent from the

Middle States and the West; and of the 186,000 Negro troops far too high a percentage was recruited from fugitives to fill technical quotas of states like Massachusetts.

This volunteer army was a remarkable organization *aside* from its fighting qualities. It had to be because of the vast extent of the disaffected area, the nature of the terrain, and the breakdown of all civil and military control. This was a situation that would have gladdened the heart of Joe Stalin with his concept of defense in depth. Three hundred regiments were used to protect communications and for garrison duty. Probably as many more were on such special, detached duties that they were under fire only a few times. Armies moving into the South had to depend largely on wagon trains. It required 2,000 wagons and 12,000 horses to carry a two day food supply for an army of 100,000 men. Wounded had to be moved by ambulance to the base, then on to the general hospitals. There were 4,000 ambulances and improvised spring wagons, operated by 10,000 horses and ten thousand men, and 204 general hospitals with 136,000 beds which handled 1,057,000 cases during the war. All of the food for the army of men and horses, all of the wounded from the field to the ambulance trains, all of the quartermasters' stores, all of the reinforcements, all of this and more passed through the base. The farther an army got from its base, the longer the wagon trains, the more exposed it was to raids and to starvation. Sherman had a supply line 500 miles long when he got to Atlanta. Grant was obliged to run eighteen trains a day from Stony Point to his army at Petersburg.

The threat to supply bases and wagon trains came first from rebel cavalry. The greatest of the rebel cavalry leaders was J. E. B. Stuart, regular army officer resigned, one of the elite of the Confederate generals, and commander of Lee's cavalry. He was the eyes of the army and on occasion an able infantry corps commander. Lighthearted and full of fun, honorable, temperate, and courageous, he lived without drinking, swearing, or wenching. He was a hard fighter but a gentleman and a worthy foe. Twice he rode around the Union army and was always a threat to its supply lines and exposed outposts until his force was overwhelmed by the equally brillant Sheridan and he was killed. Cavalry moved ahead of marching troops, protected their flanks, and guarded wagon trains. They made diversionary raids, being mounted infantry in many respects. This sort of opposition could be met in orthodox fashion. The same was not true of other cavalry leaders who were Partisan Rangers.

Partisan Rangers were legalized plunderers, authorized by the Confederate Congress, April 21, 1862. The term was never clearly defined. John B. Mosby in the Shenandoah Valley and Nathan Bedford Forrest in Mississippi and Tennessee were both in this classification, part and parcel of a general resistance movement organized by the Davis administration. Forrest was a shade closer to a regular cavalry leader than Mosby. These men organized and financed their own cavalry outfits, plundered at will and divided the spoils, operated secretly at night, hid their uniforms and posed as innocent civilians when in danger, killed and robbed much as they pleased, answerable only to the Davis government and not to field commanders such as Lee in the East and Bragg in the West. They were paid in cash for any munitions they captured. Forrest was a pre-war commercial slave trader whose troops were allowed to murder the Negro and some white soldiers captured at Fort Pillow, and who later organized the Ku Klux Klan. That he was allowed to live is evidence of the disorganized state of government after Lincoln's death. How many thousands of guerillas there were in the mountainous area is any man's guess but they were so numerous as to interfere with the conscription machinery of the Confederacy. They were thieves, robbers, and cutthroats, strongly condemned by men like Lee and Stuart and hunted relentlessly by the Union troops.

The soldiers caught on pretty fast to the fact that they were fighting something more than a gentleman's army. It took the generals a while longer. Meanwhile, the situation got completely out of hand. McClellan, Buell, and others tried to prevent their soldiers from foraging. Even an army officer should have known that peach orchards, chicken coops, and hog pens were not inviolate to soldiers who had been eating hardtack and sowbelly, especially when their owners were off fighting to break up the Union and the people back home were demanding harsh treatment for traitors. In any case, generals had to adjust their tactics to the situation. Grant started south in late 1862 with

48,000 men and had to use half of them to guard his railroad and supply depots. General Van Dorn's cavalry slipped in behind him, captured his million dollar supply base at Holly Springs, and left his army without food. Forrest roamed all over the country, cutting railroads and telegraph lines and destroying one garrison after another. Grant sent out foragers who found enough food for a half dozen armies. No Western armies ever went hungry thereafter. Grant's brilliant Vicksburg Campaign and Sherman's march to the sea followed.

More important was the acceptance of two fundamental concepts: (1) the rebellion could not be put down by trying to occupy and garrison territory; armies must be hunted down and destroyed; and (2) people who lent aid and encouragement to guerillas must accept the consequences. Even so, the war was a complicated business because of supply lines. Grant moved constantly to his left in the Wilderness Campaign in order to shift his base from one river landing to another at will and to keep his army between his base and the enemy. His advance was delayed at times to shield a wagon train some seventy miles long. He had to send Sheridan's cavalry into the Shenandoah Valley and literally take it apart because it continued to feed Lee's army, to sustain Mosby's guerillas, and to pose a constant threat not only to Washington but to couriers, supply trains, even ambulances filled with wounded and dying men.

This army of young men should have been well handled. The people wanted it that way. In retrospect it seems to have been victimized by incompetent generals, politicians, and administrators. The record is encyclopedic. The facts are devastating and cruel. The Chief of Ordnance was Brigadier-General James W. Ripley, 67 years old when the rebellion began and responsible for supplying the army with arms and ammunition. He would not approve breech-loading rifles, and it was not until he was relieved in September 1863, after the Peninsular campaign, after Antietam and Gettysburg, Bull Run and Chancellorsville, Chickamauga and Shiloh, that these improved weapons were approved. Volunteers were sent into battle in 1861-62 with muzzle loading muskets, some rifled, some smoothbore made at Springfield Armory or the Enfield Armory in England; but hundreds of thousands were given Belgian, Austrian, Prussian, even Russian muskets, all of them heavy, clumsy, inaccurate, and requiring ammunition of many kinds. The men who captured Vicksburg immediately appropriated the imported Enfields captured there for their own use. Poor guns increased the difficulty of supply, greatly reduced the fire power of the infantry, and tragically increased the mortality rate.

When men stood up in solid ranks in a meadow three hundred feet apart and fired at each other until more than half of them were on the ground some officers needed their heads examined; and, when charge after charge was ordered against solidly entrenched positions some officers heads should have rolled. Mass attacks may have been justified when muskets were used and the attack could be started from a position close to the objective, but not when rifles were used with their long range effectiveness. Let us be realistic about this business. A great deal has been written about the incompetent Burnside's slaughter of his men to no purpose and against the judgment of his corps commanders at Fredricksburg; but Lee sent his men time after time into massed artillery fire at Malvern Hill; and he refused to believe Longstreet that no 15,000 men alive could make the charge at Gettysburg until most of them lay dead and wounded. Even at the end of the war, Hood so completely slaughtered his Confederate army at Franklin and Nashville that it disintegrated, all without the slightest chance of success; and Lee kept it up at Petersburg and Five Forks while Grant was begging him to quit and his men were starving. Grant himself lost 12,000 in 30 minutes at Cold Harbor. The boys in the Union Army put a stop to this business after a while. In the East, they sat down and made coffee. Sherman's men in the West, one of the most efficient, undisciplined armies ever assembled, carried shovels on their backs and never stopped anywhere without digging trenches. If they had to stand up to load and fire their guns, they were going to stand deep enough for some degree of safety. Shiloh taught a lesson about entrenchments. Some of them did something about guns too, the Seventh Illinois and the Ninety-seventh Indiana buying their own Spencer breech loaders at $51.00 apiece. Everywhere in the armies they refused to make frontal assaults unless there was some chance of success.

It was not a matter of cowardice but of common sense. They charged at Cold Harbor but they wrote their names and home addresses on slips of paper first and pinned them on their backs. While all of this was going on, Ripley refused to approve an order for two thousand 13-inch shells charged with Greek fire, refused to approve a liquid chlorine shell which is said to have been better than the Germans used so effectively in the first World War, and rejected a breech-loading cannon which could fire a 4-pound ball one hundred times in six minutes for a distance of two and one-half miles. Three types of machine guns were available but were rejected for use. The Gatling, firing 250 shots per minute, was not adopted until after the war.

The English language fails one completely in the area of incompetent officers. One account after another tells the wretched story. It was not because they were West Point men, because McClellan, Pope, Burnside, Buell failed miserably, but Grant, Sherman, Sheridan, and Thomas were superb. Even McClellan and Hooker were great organizers and deeply concerned about the welfare of their troops. It was not because they were volunteers without professional training; the division here was about the same. Incompetence came from professional jealousy (curse of universities as well as armies), from politics, from decentralization, and more than anything else from utter inability to discover men's frailties until they are facing death. That is why the soldiers were able to evaluate them better than anyone else. They refused to salute McDowell. They called Meade a "goggle-eyed snapping turtle," and Howard "Old Prayer Book," but Sherman was Uncle Billy and Thomas was Pops. Confederate soldiers loved Lee, had enormous respect for Johnston, were afraid of Jackson. Soldiers sent officers to the rear to protect them and they sent them there because of cowardice. They requested their resignations, refused to cheer when they made their appearance. When things got too bad, they deserted. So many men died, were discharged for disability, became ill or were assigned to cooking, nursing, driving wagons, or went home that divisions shrank from 15,000 to 8,000 and regiments from 1,000 to 600.

State governments enrolled the volunteers, frequently clothed and armed men, and appointed battalion and regimental officers. The men themselves elected all company officers. Colonels, therefore, were appointed for political reasons more often than not, and upon them rested the responsibility of training the volunteers. Probably 50 per cent of the regiments were trained, if one can use the word, by incompetents. Seven per cent of the colonels were killed, 47 per cent finished the war, and 46 per cent resigned or were dismissed. Lincoln did not condone appointments or dismissals because of officers' political affiliations as shown by his tolerance of McClellan; but he could not escape giving important assignments to nationally prominent politicians, nor ignore men's attitudes toward emancipation, reconstruction, and reform programs. The army could never be divorced from the causes of the war. Nathaniel P. Banks, distinguished Speaker of the

House of Representatives at Washington and some time governor of Massachusetts, was made major-general of volunteers, given important command in Northern Virginia, and then sent to New Orleans as successor to General Benjamin Butler. His reputation as an antislavery statesman was great, his administration of the New Orleans military district was adequate, but how many men needlessly lost their lives at Cedar Mountain and Sabine Cross-roads because of his military incompetence is any man's guess.

O. O. Howard, graduate of West Point, biblical scholar and humanitarian, founder of Howard University, recipient of the Congressional Medal of Honor for bravery at Fair Oaks, was a brave man; but he did not listen to reports from his officers or obey the orders of his superior at Chancellorsville with disastrous results; he was plagued by indecision at Gettysburg, distressed by Sherman's march to the sea, and so hopelessly inefficient as Director of the Freedman's Bureau as to impair greatly the usefulness of that organization. Men had little respect for his religous fervor because he never helped them solve their personal problems. Leonidas Polk was his counterpart in the Confederate army. Episcopal bishop of Louisiana and founder of the University of the South at Sewanee, Tennessee, he was appointed by Davis for morale and psychological effect. McClernand, one of Grant's greatest problems, possessed of ambition and little tact or talent, was a Democratic Congressman when appointed colonel and then major-general. He tried desperately by intrigue to supplant Grant in the West and McClellan in the East, was charged with responsibilty for much of the heavy losses before Vicksburg, and was sent home by Grant; but he regained his command because of his status as a politician in Illinois.

Then there was the matter of clothing and food. Here was a land literally flowing with milk and honey, rich and prosperous. There was not the slightest reason why boys in the Union or Confederate armies ever should have been poorly clothed, yet untold numbers of Lee's men were barefoot and unable to march on the hard surface roads north of the Potomac, and were reduced to stripping the clothing, even underwear from Union dead on the battlefield at night. Frequently, Union men were greatly confused by advancing rebel troops clad in Union blue uniforms. Some Union soldiers were issued uniforms at the beginning of such inferior quality as simply to dissolve in the rain, and in one case the men had to stand muster draped in blankets. They were sent on to the Peninsula and into the deep South without appropriate summer clothing. Officers bought their own food, had their own mess, paid 40 cents per day for the privilege of riding government horses, and dressed fashionably which made them good marks for sharpshooters.

The South was literally bursting with food. Grant found plenty for his army, so did Sherman, but Lee had to scatter his army to feed it at times and Bragg's troops at Missionary Ridge had only parched corn and acorns in their knapsacks. It is incredible that any Confederate general should have allowed his men to go hungry. It is even more incredible that any Union soldiers should ever have been without an abundance of well cooked food. Government administrators and field commanders really had to work at being stupid to issue flour, salt pork, fresh meat, beans or hominy to soldiers and expect them to do their own cooking. Some companies, of course, had their own company cooks but there was no systematically organized food service, and when each man had to prepare his own food from flour and salt pork it is amazing that any of them lived through the ordeal. Companies, usually 60 men in strength, were the smallest unit to which supplies were issued. Cooks were selected from the ranks, each for ten days, or men were divided into groups of six to ten. Field rations were issued to each man and could be eaten raw. The hiring of Negro cooks was authorized in 1863. Salt pork was eaten raw with hardtack.

Bread was baked in cities for the Army of the Potomac. Vaults under the Capitol turned out 16,000 loaves daily for McClellan. Grant built ovens at City Point which supplied 123,000 loaves daily to his army. Hardtack was three inches square and one-half inch thick. Each man got ten each day and enough coffee for two quarts. Dessicated vegetables were cabbage, turnips, carrots, parsnips, onions, potato tops, corn stalks, pea vines pressed into cakes one foot square, one inch thick, and dried. The soldiers hated the whole nasty mess and with good reason. Baked beans were an easy favorite. No one knows why dried fruits and potatoes were not issued. Food from home came in peck boxes, postage paid by the army. Work of the sanitary commission was indispensable in the gathering of food. Despite all of this, thousands of men, for weeks on end, ate broken hardtack, wet with water, fried in a canteen with salt pork and sprinkled with sugar. Men could and did buy from the sutlers (agents of graft and corruption in any army) but prices were outrageous. Soldiers received $13.00 per month. Cheese was 80 cents per pound, condensed milk (pound can) 50 cents, canned fruit $1.00, sweet potatoes or onions 15 cents, butter 85 cents. There was some drinking, and Sherman's men were given three rations of whiskey per day after Shiloh. The men always had tobacco.

There was no uniformity about sanitation. Soldiers drank from the streams, and carried on a running battle with lice. Five men died from disease for every two who died from bullets. In August 1861, three hundred sixty-four men of every 1000 were sick, and during the war 249,000 died of sickness, with about equal numbers of 'fever', diarrhea, pneumonia and small pox, measles and other childhood ailments. No one knew what caused these diseases. Those who rose above these handicaps were as hard as nails and master workmen. They ran steamboats and railroads. Sherman's army could march two and one-half miles an hour when necessary, and build bridges, railways, and corduroy roads as fast as the army moved. Meanwhile, they could find their own food, burn everything in a radius of 50 miles, dig entrenchments, and fight battles in their spare time.

Medical service was a disgrace. Soldiers in camp, both North and South, lived under conditions likely to make them sick. Good medical care was not to be had. In many cases, they would have been better off without doctors. Bandages were not sterilized and instruments were simply wiped with rags or rinsed in a bucket of water. The United States Sanitary Commission, purely voluntary, spent $15,000,000 dollars doing what the army should have done, providing bandages, compresses, clothing, blankets, linen, and so forth. Surgeons went into the battle of Perryville without supplies and 2500 wounded lay on the field for days. At Fort Donelson, 1735 Union and 1007 Confederate soldiers lay four days without attention. No clothing, bandages, or stimulants were available to them. After Shiloh, the governors of Ohio, Illinois, and Indiana sent steamers to Pittsburg Landing for the wounded. Many incompetent doctors were brought into the service by the contract system. Fourteen per cent of the wounded died after operations. The Sanitary Commission established a system to record burials; designed hospital cars; maintained homes for soldiers traveling, with food, shelter, and medical care; helped correct irregularities in papers; helped people locate their sons in the army; distributed tobacco and writing paper.

When the armies went into winter quarters, as they had to do because of the mud, the men built log huts with fireplaces. The war was fought in the woods. They did a great deal of reading. They organized lyceums. They established schools. Baseball became popular in 1862, and as many as 300 games would be played at one time at Falmouth. They played cards and checkers. They did a great deal of writing. They had cockfights and sometimes they gambled. It is easy to overemphasize such matters as profanity, drinking, and gambling. Men came out of the army about the way they went in, no better, no worse. Every regiment had a chaplain but here as in everything else there was hopeless incompetency. Chaplains from time immemorial had been intermediaries between the armies and God. In the American Army and Navy they had been teachers and preachers. In the Civil War they combined these functions with personal service and consolation to the individual soldier, but not every chaplain was a reputable man of the cloth. No attempt was made to keep both Catholic and Protestant chaplains available to the men. Religious revivals, however, were common.

Soldiers of both armies, whether they came from the East, the North, the South, or the West, have left us an imperishable and unmistakable record in their letters, in their diaries, and in their songs: a record of terrible loneliness. Music played a tremendously important part in their lives whether on the march or around the campfires. We know what they sang: the majestic *Battle Cry of Freedom* and *Battle Hymn of the Republic* of course; but the one song heard more than any other was

Weeping Sad and *Lonely* and close behind in popularity *Tenting on the Old Camp Ground, Just Before the Battle Mother,* and *When Johnny Comes Marching Home,*—all embracing death, family ties, indescribable sadness. Above all and universal in both armies was *Home, Sweet Home.*

These boys had toiled over mountains, through dense forests, and in seas of mud. They had suffered both hunger and thirst. They knew the tortures of freezing cold and blistering heat. They had walked into the face of death so often that the only fear left was fear of failure or cowardice. Yet, in those awful, restless, hours at night before impending battles, they wrote not of their own ills, or perils, or fears, but in the most tender concern for the welfare of those at home.

Their material comforts were neglected. Their spiritual life was almost ignored. They were called upon to perform feats beyond the limits of human endurance. If captured, they emerged from prison naked, emaciated, dirty, sometimes insane, unable to walk or to remember their names or regiments. If killed, they were buried in their blankets, usually where they fell by their buddies if they could get to the battlefield, with wooden headboards bearing their names. Thousands were never properly buried, untold thousands were never identified. Facing death, they found the deepest meaning of life—great souls must walk alone. They died and the armies moved on, leaving them even in death to their own resources, as lonely as they had been in the last tragic years of their youth.

IV

RESPONSIBILITIES OF POWER

Great in its wrath and great in its forgiveness. Strong in its will to live and determined to erase the blot of human bondage from its bounds. That purpose of the nation emerged slowly but with clarity during the first year of Lincoln's Administration. Neither complete unity nor understanding were to be expected in the beginning. They were highly desirable, never fully attained, but the twin objectives were finally achieved by the army. The rebellion against Federal authority was crushed—the nation lived—and slavery was abolished.

What constitutes a nation? Lincoln said in his message to Congress, December 2, 1862: "A nation may be said to consist of its territory, its people, and its laws." With regard to territory, he gave his now famous description of an inseparable nation: "That portion of the earth's surface," he said, "which is owned and inhabited by the people of the United States is well adapted to be the home of one national family; and it is not well adapted for two or more. . . . There is no line, straight or crooked, suitable for a national boundary upon which to divide." Then, having described the vast interior of the country and its outlets to the sea through New York, New Orleans, and San Francisco, he said: "These outlets, east, west, and south, are indispensable to the well-being of the people inhabiting and to inhabit this vast interior region. Which of the three may be best is no proper question. All are better than either, and all of right belong to that people and to their successors forever. True to themselves, they will not ask where a line of separation shall be, but will vow rather that there shall be no line." When Lincoln wrote these words, Vicksburg alone obstructed the free passage of commerce by way of the Mississippi to the sea, and the fall of Vicksburg was not far away.

Lincoln never had any reason to doubt the steadfastness of the army on this point. Those men who went off to war had a purpose. They had the same thing on their minds as their people at home. They loved life; they loved personal freedom; they loved the Union. "If words had meaning, then the Declaration spoke the language of freedom, and the only bond of union they recognized as superior to the Constitution was the virtue and moral power of a free people. They never should have been told that slavery, not liberty, constituted the bonds of Union, and that they could not keep one without the other. The Union was theirs by virtue of a warranty deed from Heaven, and they expected to keep it by advocating what they believed to be justice, righteousness and truth." The boys who went off to war expected to keep it by dying if necessary. Some of them hardly knew how to load a rifle when thrust into battle. They were boys today, men tomorrow, civilians one day, soldiers the next, veterans in a matter of hours. Some ran away of course and a great many died but mostly they stood and fought valiantly until exhausted, rested and fought again.

An army of a million men is something to think about. It has power. It has will. It has purpose. It can be crippled and beaten back, but it can not be destroyed except by attrition, by loss of faith, or by incompetent leadership. Lincoln's army was not defeated. It always had men and equipment. It never lost faith in itself or its country. Neither the preservation of the Union, nor the abolition of slavery, nor yet the suppression of vindictiveness and cruel retribution could have been achieved save for the army. It could have and probably would have done anything Lincoln asked it to do. The thing he never wanted was hatred, vindictiveness, punishment. The word "people" was the important one in his trilogy of national attributes.

The people continued to be uppermost in his thoughts. He had dwelt upon this in his first inaugural, saying: "We are not enemies but friends. We must not be enemies. Though passion may have strained, it must not break our bonds of affection. The mystic chords of memory, stretching from every battlefield and patriot grave to every living heart and hearthstone all over this land, will yet swell the chorus of the Union when again touched, as surely they will be, by the better angels of our nature." These were not empty words by a man who knew war was inevitable. Not at all! There was presently in the nation a great pall of darkness and despair, hatred and divided counsels. Lincoln was thinking of peace, not victory, of mutual confidence and understanding in solution of the nation's problems. He was correct in his hopes, wrong in his appraisals. This is the kindest possible interpretation which can be placed upon his pronouncements and his actions. He was determined to retake Federal forts which had been seized and to restore Federal authority in rebellious areas. How else could it be done except by armed force? Did he underestimate the extent of the rebellion and the intensity of hatred? Surely not, but if he did not, then he failed to understand the crippling effect of slavery upon the character and intelligence of the oppressor, and upon the habits of a slaveholding community.

The four ensuing years were destined to be perilous and sorrowful years for Lincoln, for the people, and above all for the men on the battlefield, simply because the men who were rebelling were neither rational nor reasonable. The whole business was born in hatred and fear. There was no sanity about it, nor love of country, nor repentance about generations of oppression. Consider the facts.

Lincoln had been elected by correct Constitutional procedures, and these men were rebelling against the authority of the Federal government because of his election. There was nothing in this kindly man's entire private and public life incompatible with the best in the nation's traditions. His love of humanity, his faith in democratic processes, his hopes for future generations are not open to impeachment. He qualifies by every test as a leader in the cause of enlightenment. Yet few men in public life have been so vilified, before taking office, and by men engaged in treasonable enterprises. He was accused of "ill-timed jocularity," of "pusillanimous evasion of responsibility," of "vulgar pettifoggery," of "disgusting levity." He was called an "Abolition orangoutang." He was said to be profoundly ignorant of the "institutions of the Republic." He was dishonest and cowardly, said men whose success would have destroyed Constitutional government, done great damage to a growing and prosperous nation, and doomed to perpetual slavery three and one-half million persons and their descendants.

The men who were doing this knew precisely what they were doing. The masses were deceived but not their leaders. They tried to avoid the stigma of treason by claiming authority of states which they did not control, by authority from a people who were hopelessly confused as to issues, and by force which was totally destructive of the rights of individuals they claimed to be protecting. There was not a single new idea in their whole theory of government. They conveniently forgot all about Calhoun's doctrine of concurrent majority when it came to adopting a constitution. They closed their eyes to the specter of state rights. They lost all claim to independent sovereignty by continuing to operate under the Constitution of the United States. The whole business was a colossal fabrication foisted upon the people and future historians by citizens of the United States who were violating their obligations of allegiance.

They were victimizing, actually ruining, an entire population of citizens of the United States in one area by forcing them to fight against their government, stealing their property, depreciating their currency, and cutting them off from their friends, relatives, and business relationships in the rest of the country. They killed or sold into slavery Negroes in their country's uniforms, which they themselves had once proudly worn and then betrayed. They threatened with death the white commanders of Negro troops. They encouraged and tried to defend subversives and spies, bushwhackers, bridge-burners, marauders, guerrillas, partisan rangers, and irregulars of all sorts who were crippling the efforts of the United States government to restore order. Their House of Representatives resolved that the Confederate government ought to demand the release of all persons who were "taken prisoner while in armed and active hostility to the United States although not regularly enrolled or enlisted in the Confederate army." The audacity of men in rebellion on this point almost defies belief, except that they were equally guilty and feared the establishment of precedents with regard to summary punishments. General Braxton Bragg addressed General H. G. Wright from Murfreesboro, on December 1, 1862, on the subject of political prisoners who had been confined for disloyal acts, in the following bitter language: "It is not to be denied that the patience of the Confederate Government is becoming threadbare. . . . Union—social association with a people guilty of such acts [detaining subversives]—is henceforth an impossibility. Destitution, the prison—death itself—is preferable." This was not a defense of the right of revolution; they never claimed as much. It was not a defense of state authority because no state had claimed any power that had been denied. It was treason, criminal subversion, indescribable hatred. The war intensified the bitterness, created new hatreds, which Lincoln with his heart of incomparable compassion never ceased trying to allay. He had the full cooperation of his two greatest generals, Grant and Sherman.

The war had not yet begun, really, when the incomparable Grant, untried, unknown, object of jealousy and intrigue by his superior, captured Fort Donelson, thereby piercing the frontier defenses of the Confederates in the West. The country was electrified by the victory, even more by his demand of unconditional surrender. Here was a man who was soon to demonstrate an iron will and tenacity in pursuit of victory, but the most significant action at Donelson, often overlooked, was his instruction to his men to do nothing which would humiliate the prisoners because they "are our own countrymen." Nothing was done. The captured General Buckner complained about the lack of attention to the needs of thousands of men and Grant gave him authority to look after them. Many stole horses and escaped. Grant told Halleck it was less of a job to take them than to keep them. The wounded of both armies were mixed up without any means of identification and sent off to hospitals. Then for a time no one could find Buckner. Officers were sent north with their sidearms. This became a common practice. There was a long period in which some captured officers stayed in hotels in Columbus, Ohio, wandered about the city armed, and on one occasion were given seats of honor in the state legislature. One general was comfortably located in a hotel in Baltimore. Other officers roamed the streets of Washington and Memphis. They had 200 slaves with them in Camp Chase at Columbus and others in camp in St. Louis. At Fort Columbus in the East they complained because they did not have servants at meal time and no one to do their shopping or clean their rooms, and the letter of complaint went as high as the Secretaries of War and State with endorsements along the way.

The problem of handling prisoners of war, political prisoners, paroled Union soldiers, and deserters was difficult; and conflicts of authority were very confusing; but neither was a satisfactory explanation for young ladies bringing 'raspberries' to prisoners, or the issuing of so much food that prisoners could sell some of it back to the commissary. Officers who were exchanged were in many cases allowed to purchase new uniforms and to wear their side arms; privates were given Union uniforms, and these together with those captured or stolen from the dead, confused the Union armies no end on the battlefield. Lee, fighting desperately to feed and clothe his men insisted they had a right to wear Union uniforms and the United States government allowed itself to be intimidated in the matter.

Grant's powerful lieutenant, William T. Sherman, prosecuted the war vigorously, carrying its rigors into the heartland of the rebellion and bringing it home to the people by fire and sword, burning public buildings, factories, and palatial homes. He was as relentless as Grant in pursuit of victory but equally conscious of the responsibility of power. There came a day in March, 1865, when Grant and Sherman were closing in a vise the remnants of Lee's army of Virginia and the weary men of Johnston. Lincoln and Sherman and Grant talked at the latter's headquarters on the James, the generals deeply impressed by Lincoln's desire for a generous peace. Grant's terms of surrender to Lee were never criticized. Sherman's terms to Johnston, made a few days after Lincoln's assassination, were so generous as to be disallowed by the Secretary of War. "In general terms," said Sherman, "the war to cease; a general amnesty, so far as the Executive of the United States can command, on condition of the disbandment of the Confederate armies, the distribution of the arms, and the resumption of peaceful pursuits by the officers and men hitherto composing the armies." Veterans of the battlefield were speaking here; so, too, was Lincoln, and in a very real sense, the people. Yet, there was something very naive about it all.

Passing from the battlefield to the political arena, we find Lincoln's policy equally revealing. His theory, from first to last, was that the nation was intended to be perpetual. All ordinances of secession were held to be null and void, and state governments which had passed such ordinances to have fallen into the hands of disloyal elements. His theory was correct. This was a rebellion against Federal authority which could not be suppressed by ordinary processes. It had been put down by force of arms and at terrific cost. But the very cost of putting it down, in broken homes and ruined lives, in destruction of property, in lasting hatreds, in loss of that faith which is the basis of all our institutional life, added up to a monumental responsibility which overshadowed and took precedence before all else. It was here that Lincoln's theories were wrong, and here that he failed—always remembering, of course, that the failure was in having confidence in the righteousness of men whose past conduct did not warrant it; and always remembering, also, that his untimely death was one of the cruel imponderables of history.

Lincoln's theory that state governments had fallen into the hands of subversive elements was followed by two conclusions on his part: (1) that such states were out of their proper relation to the Union; and (2) since the Chief Executive possessed the power to pardon, the authority to reestablish state governments was in his hands. Both conclusions are open to serious doubt. The states as such forfeited all claims to the privileges and protection guaranteed to them by the Constitution when they refused to abide by the results of the election of 1860, passed ordinances of secession, created a new government, made war upon the Constitution and Government of the United States. One of the privileges they had enjoyed was to maintain an aristocracy with extraordinary political power in the nation. A second one was to hold in absolute bondage a large portion of their inhabitants. Can it be argued that they were entitled to retain such privileges, the existence of which had causd a bloody civil war. Of course not! Take the case then of individuals. Even forget the charge of treason on which every one of them was assuredly open to trial. All were guilty of resisting with arms the enforcement of the laws, of engaging in riotous acts, of obstructing the mails, of desecrating the flag, and so forth. None was tried, none was convicted, therefore none could be pardoned. If an executive can do this, then there is no law. Extension of amnesty to a large group of people is one thing; to do this and make exception is quite another. Then to select from the exceptions, purely on the basis of secret documents, those who might come back into full political rights and call it pardon, is to make a complete mockery of government by law. The question here is whether the power to suspend the operation of the law in specific cases was included in the pardoning power; but far beyond any question of constitutional authority is the question of far-reaching public policy.

Historians have focused their attention upon the disagreement between President Lincoln and his successor President Johnson to the neglect of a very important point. Both possessed the pardoning power and exercised it lavishly. It is easy to point to the exceptions they made in their general amnesty proclamations, and the requirements that high military and naval officers, civil officials, persons who had formerly taken an oath to support the Constitution and then made war upon it, and those possessed of $20,000 worth of property must make individual application for pardon. The truth of the matter is that securing a pardon became a sort of game at which the petitioner never lost because these men, (some 18,000) were adept at fabricating all sorts of excuses, obtaining supporting testimonials, and keeping the documents classified as confidential and away from the prying eyes of historians for almost one hundred years. Almost as bad in its consequences was the fact that these pardons restored to the recipients all property which had been confiscated and from which the emancipated slaves were now driven unless they consented to a state of peonage. It was ruinous to thousands who had begun a new life under the guidance and authority of military men like Sherman; and it destroyed in one fell stroke the splendid beginnings of social and economic reconstruction endorsed by Secretary Stanton and carried out by the benevolent societies.

Finally, President Lincoln's policy established two additional precedents. He suggested to the military governor of Louisiana, and President Johnson suggested to the military governor of Mississippi the advisability of extending the franchise to a few literate and property holding people of color. Expediency, not principle, was to be the rule. The second precedent had to do with reconstruction of state governments, in which a number of voters equal to one-tenth the votes cast in the election of 1860 and being qualified voters under the election laws of that date might proceed with reconstruction of state governments. The stage was now set for continued subordination of the former slaves by the white population, once it was free from army control and had a renewed voice in the government at Washington. There is no evidence here of any intention to come to grips with the two great political evils: foisting upon the nation political power derived from oppression, and compelling millions of people to obey laws which they had no part in making. They knew better. How well the country knew! Thomas Branagan had warned them in 1805 in prophetic words: "The tyrants of the South gain an ascendency over the citizens of the North, and enhance their paramount rights of suffrage and sovereignty accordingly as they enslave and subjugate sons of Africa. ... Unless this villainous inequality is in time remedied, the rights and liberties of our citizens will be eventually swallowed up."

There were those who turned away from reality in 1861. They had wanted peace by compromise. They had wanted a war of limited objectives. They had been willing to enter into compromises which would barter away forever the high prerogatives of the people to determine public policy in respect to human rights. They had been willing to place a premium upon resort to arms by men who had lost a decision at the ballot box. They had been willing to recognize the power of a section to restrain the whole of the nation. Not so the men—those much maligned radicals—who had put their hands to the task of restoring the authority and prestige of Constitutional government. Refusal to compromise was a great triumph of democracy. It saved Constitutional government in the United States. The men who tried to break up the Union gambled that secession would be peaceable and lost. Lincoln had refused to make any compromises after his election. He had been compelled to use armed force to restore the authority of the government, but the compromisers were still in the Union. Some of them were in high places. Lincoln was not one of them, but Andrew Johnson had been, and George B. McClellan also. Both men were deeply involved in what happened.

There is a school of thought which holds that until the summer of 1862 a settlement without much change in institutional life was possible. They say the character of the war changed; that it became a revolution, a hard, harsh, cruel war, one that demanded victories and dealt roughly with anything like slavery and anybody like McClellan who stood in the way of complete victory. This theory simply does not fit the facts. The first shot shattered the institution of slavery beyond recovery. It was not then a question of whether slavery would be abolished but of whether it would be restored. Lincoln had refused to be hurried into a premature Emancipation Proclamation; but, when it came, it was a public pronouncement to the people of this country, to foreign nations, and in a very real sense to those in rebellion that complete freedom for the slaves merely awaited restoration of Federal authority. The happenstance that thirty-four year old McClellan had a distorted conception of the conflict does not alter the facts.

It was possible for Lincoln to overlook his gratuitous insults, but he could not ignore his failure to use his army to the full extent of its power nor his flagrant intrusion into matters of state. Three times he turned away from golden opportunities to destroy Lee's army. He virtually courted dismissal, and unquestionably would have been punished severely by many a government, by demanding that slavery must not be disturbed in any particular. Lincoln had warned him time and again that he was under a cloud of suspicion, that responsible people were charging him with procrastination bordering on treason, and that he must cease temporizing. It has been said that McClellan was obsessed with the idea that he must save his army to save the Union. This again is very doubtful. He left his army to fight its own way across the Peninsula to a new base and took refuge on a river boat; refused to allow his corps commanders to move on Richmond when there was every prospect of success; failed to take the initiative when Lee's army was shattered at Malvern Hill; and allowed him to escape destruction at Antietam. It was then that he had to go, in the fateful autumn of 1862. He stood at the very brink of treason when he gathered his associates around him to discuss his obligation to oppose publicly, perhaps with the army, the Emancipation Proclamation. How lucky the man was to have escaped unscathed, for his friends rebuked him, his Commander-in-Chief dismissed him, and in the end the country repudiated him. Yet, this was the man who was the choice of the great and powerful Democratic party in the election of 1864.

He stood on a platform of compromise and repudiation of the very things for which his own men had died; and the Republican party, the anti-slavery party, the party of the Higher Law, the party of nationalism, felt called upon to nominate as Lincoln's running-mate a strong state rights man from the area in rebellion. Andrew Johnson became President when Lincoln was assassinated, still loyal to the Union, but utterly oblivious to the fact that three hundred thousand of the nation's youth had died to purge their country of a great moral wrong, that a powerful revolution in human institutions had swept through the land, that the Union as he had known it was no more. It was at this point that the revolution died. All that was to be accomplished had been accomplished by the army. When it stacked its arms the contest for human rights came to an end. Emancipation had been sublime in its prospects, awful in its execution.

There never was any possibility that slavery could be resurrected. The several Acts of Congress, the Emancipation Proclamation, and the Thirteenth Amendment merely confirmed an accomplished fact and put it beyond reversal by courts or a later Congress. The trouble was that those who saw the enormity of the problem, the fearful responsibility that faced the country, the glorious opportunity to erect a lasting monument to the dead, were so few in number as to be treated with the same disdain as was visited upon the early antislavery men. We struck the chains from the limbs of men and called it freedom. Silence came on the battlefield and we called it peace. But slavery, as we have said, was something more than holding a person as a chattel, and giving a man his freedom involved something more than calling him into one's living room and telling him that he was free to go where he pleased. Slavery was something more than the legal bondage of three and one-half million men, women, and children. Slavery was a firm, universal, and irreversible belief by the whites of the rebellious area that the people of color were biologically unequal and 'racially' inferior to themselves, and the application of that belief to the relationships of all kinds between individuals and between the whole of each group in society. Slavery was a denial of the natural rights of man.

The South at the close of the war was a spiritual and political vacuum. The men who had carried the burden of government at Washington through four agonizing years knew that it would be a wicked and cowardly thing to withdraw its control from the South. They knew that Congressional withdrawal would mean government of the old slave states by and for the whites for a long time. They knew that if the nation did not make decisions the Southern whites would make them, and that tomorrow would play no part in their scheme of things, only present humiliation and the delusion of past glory. They knew that the protecting mantle of the Federal Constitution must be thrown over these newly emancipated people; that denial of the right of secession was too moderate a restraint upon the delusion of state sovereignty; and that the burden of proof must rest upon those who had forfeited the public trust, in all matters pertaining to the restoration of their political privileges.

It is a false notion that internal peace required acceptance of these men back into the councils of the nation at the earliest practical moment. Men can pay too high a price for peace. Where else ever were men who attempted to destroy a nation allowed to come back and help govern it after 300,000 men had died to thwart their treason. This was a return to the old immorality of concession. What was the most important issue in this crisis of the war's end: the political privileges of the rebellious whites or the natural rights of three and one-half milion people who had been rescued from their oppression? Some men knew the correct answer but their prodigious efforts always fell a little short of providing complete emancipation for the people of color and redemption of democracy in the former slave states.

Freedom for the slaves came by force. It was an incomplete freedom as antislavery men had known it would be unless achieved by voluntary action and repentance and followed by retributive justice on the part of the slaveholders and the entire white population. Slaveholders never had been willing to discuss emancipation; they were no more willing now to consider emancipation in its broader aspects. They accepted the abolition of slavery because there was no other choice, but they would not admit it to have been an evil nor abandon the psychological basis on which it had rested. They were not ready to acknowledge the natural rights of people of color as persons or their Constitutional rights as citizens. They were not willing to abandon any of the legal distinctions based upon color; to recognize the right of these people to go where they pleased, marry whom they pleased, work as they pleased; to allow them free access to the courts, voting rights, office-holding; to allow them to make decisions; in short, to permit them to live otherwise than as a subservient minority. The freedmen were as free as the free persons of color had been in the slave states before 1860. They had toiled out their lives. They had only hope. The whites had robbed them of the returns from their labor; they now set about robbing them of the vision of better things. If the whites were impoverished by the war, the freedmen were more so and in no way to blame; but the whites had no sense of retributive justice either in payment for past services or assistance for the future.

Preservation of the Union was achieved by force. Preservation of the Union and restoration of the old Union were two different things. The old Union could not be restored. There had been a revolution in human institutions. Restoration of the old Union ran counter to abolition of slavery, already an accomplished fact. Men accepted its preservation but grudgingly and under duress. Love for the Union and respect for the government were hard to come by. The Lincoln policy of generosity to rebels did not evoke in return generosity to friends of the government or loyalty on the part of the rebels. It simply did not work. It was a failure. Pardons evoked impudence and defiance. Concession was regarded as evidence of fear. Once men found out they were not going to be shot, or imprisoned, or exiled, they quickly threatened ultimate vengeance. Intolerance increased by the hour. People who had remained loyal were spoken of derisively as scalawags and Northerners as carpetbaggers. Men who had waged bitter war soon returned to power. They were heroes. They had done no wrong. They hated the Union more in 1865 than in 1861 and they still believed slavery to be the best condition for the people of color. They went on living in the past and nursed their hatred. The people of color continued to suffer. People thought of themselves, spoke of themselves, as Southerners. There was almost a complete lack of national sentiment. The Confederate flag was prominently displayed through the years, more often than not with more respect than the Stars and Stripes. In short, sectionalism in all its virulence remained to plague the nation. It was hostile to social revolution and to national unity. Its evil genius was second class citizenship for people of color. It thrived on cultural deficiencies and nourished pride in second rate achievement. Certainly there is something wrong with the mental processes of historians who condemn the harshness of Congressional reconstruction and ignore depravity of Southern whites in this area of human relationships. What one historian has called a great miracle was in reality a great humiliation.

V

THE POWER TO OPPRESS

Conclusion of Congressional reconstruction ushered in another century of misrule, oppression, and violence in the area of slavery and rebellion. The situation was more sinister than it had been before the war because the former slaves were now citizens of the United States. Every act of injustice toward any one of them was a direct challenge to every citizen of the United States and to the Federal government. The situation in that respect was indeed ominous. The white people of the rebellious area still were determined that it should remain a white man's country. People of color should never be allowed to have equality of rights or a voice in political affairs. They must remain an inferior people and their control must remain decentralized. That was and is the life-giving germ of state rights: the power to oppress, the power to control in the states the rights of free persons of color. This could be done only by escaping the national conscience and by preventing protection of those people by Congress.

Slavery had been considered a matter of grave national concern. How much more so were the personal and Constitutional rights of citizens! Slavery had obstructed and confused the operations of both Houses of Congress in determination of public policy. It had struck down freedom of speech, press, and assembly at the South and had done great damage in that respect in other areas of the nation. Men in high position in government, education, and religion had been reared in its atmosphere and carried its philosophy into formulation of policy. The peace of Northern communities had been disrupted by intrusion of slaveholders or their emissaries. It had obstructed communication and travel in its strongholds of citizens from elsewhere. It had greatly damaged the image of the United States in other nations. Not only did all of this continue to be true after the war but other malign influences were added and the whole of it still exists at the end of another century. Is there anyone who would argue otherwise?

A great war had raged across the land to destroy the Union and the Constitution, against freedom and in the interest of slavery. The rebellion had failed, the Union and Constitution had been preserved, and slavery had been abolished. Common sense indicated that men at this point should examine the structure of the Union and try to repair the parts which had been weakened or needed strengthening to resist another such catastrophe. Certainly one of the requirements was that every means by which oppression had been sustained, everything that stood in the way of complete freedom for the slave, be swept away. All pretentions to state sovereignty had to be buried with the bones of the Confederacy.

Men knew that the people of the former slave states would prevent complete fulfillment of emancipation. They had worked at it during the war and they were at it vigorously before the sound of battle died away: killing, intimidating, starving the Negroes who were struggling against entanglements of the chains of former servitude. They would continue by law and by violence to keep them docile. Civil rights had proved highly vulnerable to violation during the crusade for freedom because local governments would not protect but would abuse persons who were disliked in the community. Congressional leaders, therefore, took those principles which they believed always to have been deeply embedded in the philosophy of the nation and wrote them into the Constitution. The purpose was to throw the protective mantle of the Constitution over the former slaves; to bring the full power of the Federal government and through it of the national conscience to bear upon the never-ending task of securing to every person his or her natural rights, the equal protection of the laws, and the operation of every safeguard known to the administration of justice.

The Thirteenth Amendment was intended to abolish physical restraints upon the slaves and with it a complexity of legal and racial concepts. It was intended to guarantee the natural rights of all persons by written constitutional provision, by judicial processes, and by Congressional legislation. It was the culmination of the antislavery effort to abolish all restraints upon free persons of color. It was the answer to black codes, mob violence, and denial of free enquiry and discussion. It was a clear affirmation of Congressional power to abolish slavery in all its subtle refinements. Congress followed the Thirteenth Amendment with the Civil Rights Act. This was comprehensive legislation for the protection of the individual citizen. Congress then framed the Fourteenth Amendment to remove forever any denial of national power to protect the civil rights of individuals. They said here that all persons born in this country were citizens of the United States, equal in all respects, entitled to security of their natural rights by the Federal government, and to all the safeguards of due process and equal protection of the laws regardless of anything a state might try to do or fail to do. No state government was going to be allowed to violate these natural rights of citizens of the United States, and no citizen was going to be allowed to do so even if a state failed to restrain or protect. Anyone who believes otherwise has failed to read the mountain of antislavery records and Congressional debates or has read them to no purpose.

Congress, meanwhile, placed ten of the states involved in the rebellion under military rule to maintain order, protect the freedmen and friends of the Union, and safeguard the slow process of restoring civil government. It created an agency commonly known as the Freedman's Bureau to aid the former slaves; to provide food, medical service, and education; to supervise their contractual relations with the whites; and to secure justice in the courts. Congress also specified certain definite procedures for writing new state constitutions and for the recognition of new state governments including the final step of seating Senators and Representatives in Congress. It rested its case on temporary military rule and universal manhood suffrage. It expected—the future rested—upon a contrite and cooperative spirit in the former slave states and upon a wholly new approch to national problems by Southern members of Congress. What other basis could there possibly have been for no punishments, personal or political.

The Congressional program, far from being extreme, proved to be wholly inadequate. If public policy ever was determined on a basis of faith, hope and charity, this was the time. There was precious little realism involved. A permanent department of government to protect and aid the former slaves should have been established with a director of Cabinet rank. The entire resources of the Federal government should have been committed to whatever extent was required to establish a complete educational system of public schools, colleges, and universities; to give homesteads to the former slaves; to provide vocational training for employment; and, to protect them in all their rights as citizens. There was ample precedent and a world of experience for these things in the earlier programs of gradual emancipation, in the work of the old abolition societies of the convention period, and in the program urged by Benjamin Franklin in Washington's first administration. The Freedman's Bureau tried to do these things, but it was a temporary agency without assured permanence, trained personnel, or pre-established objectives. It was abolished before its potential usefulness could be tested and the freedmen were abandoned to a hostile white population.

In retrospect, then, everything hinged upon force. The only reformation worth while was achieved through the reconstruction governments of the states which fell when the army was withdrawn. Southern whites were now free to go to work on the person of color, to destroy his manhood again, to teach him never to aspire to equality of rights or to a voice in political affairs, to make him an inferior person and make him like it. What a base falsehood it is and perversion of history to say this was the result of the excesses of reconstruction governments and military rule! The reign of terror instituted by Southern whites was started to keep emancipation to the narrowest possible limits. Brutality was born of slavery and the desire to continue slavery, and when men like President Hayes declared that justice for the Negro was to be best attained by trusting Southern whites all hope was gone. That was precisely what the war was about. We had made the complete circle and were back at the starting point because all of the injustices about to be visited upon the people of color added up to an incomplete freedom. It was peace at any price.

The Congressional program in all its outward features rested upon years of discussion. It was not something improvised for political advantage or for punishment. Men had argued passionately for well over forty years, though not always with success, that there were no distinctions of color in any of the foundation principles or basic documents of the nation; that all persons born or naturalized in the United States were citizens; that all persons are equal in the endowment of rights and are entitled to equality under the law and in the administration of justice; and that the United States, demanding allegiance, must protect its citizens in the enjoyment of their natural rights. In fact there had been a strong and it would seem irrefutable argument that since slaves must give allegiance to the United States and could be punished for treason, the Federal government must protect them in their natural endowment of rights by setting them free. The Constitutional Amendments were written in broad terms. They were written in defense of man's natural rights. They did not give anyone any thing because nothing can be given where every thing has previously been taken away. They were a Constitutional recognition of equality in the endowment, security, and exercise of rights. When slavery was abolished by the Thirteenth Amendment, the states lost the right to deny the franchise again to citizens of the United States. The courts should have so held and probably would have done so had cases been properly presented.

The first mistake, then, was in not making certain that the people of color were allowed to vote. Emancipation failed to a marked degree because we allowed the color of a man's skin to determine his civil and political rights. Freedom and participation in public affairs are complimentary. If a man's voice can not be heard in the determination of public policy then he is no longer free. It is a denial of justice. It is a foolish disregard of security. It is a complete denial of the principle of consent of the governed. It is taxation without representation. It is a violation of equal rights. It is, in the case of the United States versus its citizens, a maintenance of an oligarchy based upon color. People of color, throughout our history, have been refused many times the right to vote and hold office. They did not often serve in legislatures, in Congress, or on the bench. Great care was taken where they were allowed the franchise to reduce to a minimum their chances of being elected to office and they were seldom appointed. This was an outrage of the first magnitude. Governments derive their just power from the consent of the governed. The Declaration of Independence said so. The Constitution says nothing about color. Why then should any law? The Constitution guarantees the privileges and immunities of all citizens of the United States. Immunity is exemption from unequal burdens. If living under a government in which one has no voice is not an unequal burden, what is it?

There are many arguable reasons why people of color should have been guaranteed the franchise by the Federal government after the Civil War. The first reason is reciprocity of allegiance and protection. Bearing arms in defense of one's country and in support of one's government is the strongest possible guarantee of the right to exercise the franchise.

People of color fought in the Revolution and those who were slaves were given their freedom in return. They were citizens in most states and voted. They fought valiantly in the War of 1812 and continued to vote. They were enrolled in the army by order of Lincoln's Emancipation Proclamation to the number of 186,000 and fought courageously for the Union. White men went south to destroy the Union, slaves came north to save it and by so doing became a part of the body politic by precedent and by right. The second reason they were entitled to the franchise was because they paid taxes and denial of the franchise was taxation without representation. There are those who say the slave was represented before the war. If so it was to the degree that he was a member of his master's household and was represented in the same sense as the master's wife and children. He stepped out of that category when he became free and representation through the ballot box became essential. Because it was denied to him, more people were taxed without representation than the entire population at the time of the Revolution.

These people were entitled to the franchise, also, because the test of suffrage is manhood. All men are equal in the sense that they inherit the same rights and governments exist to protect these rights. The just powers of government are derived from the people who are governed. No man or group or class of men has a right to push other men aside and tell them they can not participate. There is no divine dispensation or grant of power to do such a thing. The people of color had to have the franchise as a guarantee of freedom. The ballot box is an impregnable fortress of liberty. The franchise is a powerful weapon in the hands of men. It can be used as easily as guns to destroy men who do not have it. Generations of white men in Europe and here in America fought for it. Every man in a state of nature has a right of self-defense. Civil government relieves him of the necessity of exercising it by guaranteeing his protection and giving him the ballot. Deny him the ballot and his right of self defense is his only recourse. A government which takes away the one without substituting the other is inviting restlessness, disquietude of unpredictable proportions, and revolution. The slave states were allowed to keep on saying who could vote and they kept the people of color from voting. Control of the franchise by state governments has created so many ridiculous situations as to be beyond the pale of respectabilty. In this case it was tragic.

Freedom for the slaves automatically gave to a people fresh from the wars of rebellion an increase of representation in Congress. The old evil of giving men extraordinary power in the government of the United States as a reward for oppressing and exploiting their fellow men was now compounded. White people in the slave states had 17 to 25 more votes in Congress than their numbers gave them any right to have before the Civil War. Approximately two and one-half million citizens of the United States in New York and Pennsylvania had sixty-four members of the House and Senate in Congress and an equal number of citizens in eight slave states had 100 members. Slavery could have been restricted, and the Fugitive Slave Act could have been repealed, if this excessive political power of slave states had not existed. There probably would never have been a civil war. It allowed one slaveholder after another to be President of the United States. Freedom for the slaves compounded the evil. Take for example the year 1910. Seven former slave states with 6,357,000 white people had seventy-nine members of the House and Senate. California, Michigan, and Connecticut with the same number of people voting without distinction of color, had thirty-five members; and New York and Ohio with 13,888,000 had sixty-nine members.

Congress sought to prevent this by writing into the Amendments authorization for a reduction in representation of any state denying the franchise, and in proportion as they did so, to any portion of its citizens on the basis of race, color, or previous condition of servitude. It was a feeble, unintelligent, almost criminal approach to the problem; first, because there were other ways of doing the disfranchising; and, second, because the states could disfranchise the Negro forever by accepting a reduction in representation. Fortunately the vagaries of politics prevented it from ever being applied. Southern whites excluded Negroes from the ballot-box, appropriated to themselves all representation based upon the Negro population, and went back to Congress to thwart any corrective legislation through the years. The result is that there has never been an honest election in the Black Belt within the lifetime of any man now alive.

Few people realize the tremendous power the final settlement gave to the dominant whites in the former area of rebellion. Their power was so great that both parties vied for its support either directly or by indirection. They did not need to nullify the Acts of Congress as they had done in 1832, they found a perfect application of nullification in the Senatorial filibuster and in committee chairmanships based on seniority. They gave up the right of a state to secede but they clung with intense fanaticism to the doctrine of state rights. They went back to Congress with increased powers to protect their right to keep on oppressing the people of color. They began to do inside the government what they had not been able to do outside. They could not determine policy but they could control by obstruction. What they did was to prevent Congress from protecting the people of color.

Everyone should read and ponder the words of Chief Justice John Marshall: "If the legislatures of the several states may, at will, annul the judgments of the courts of the United States, and destroy the rights acquired under those judgments, the Constitution itself becomes a solemn mockery; and the nation is deprived of the means of enforcing its laws by the instrumentality of its own tribunals." They should read also the proclamation of President Andrew Jackson when South Carolina nullified an Act of Congress: "I consider, then, the power to annul a law of the United States, assumed by one state, incompatible with the existence of the Union, contradicted expressly by the letter of the Constitution, unauthorized by its spirit, inconsistent with every principle on which it was founded, and destructive of the great object for which it was formed."

John C. Calhoun's idea of giving a state the power to nullify or cancel out a law of the United States is something to think about. It is still floating around to confuse the unsophisticated politician. How could it possibly have survived the hammer blow of President Jackson's proclamation, the verdict of the Civil War battlefields, and the damage done to it within the Confederacy itself? It did survive because the enemies of good government applied it within the framework of the Federal government rather than through the agency of a state government. No need to confront the power of the nation with the feeble power of a state. No need to defy an act of Congress. Keep the bill from coming to a vote and there would never be a law to argue about. It was so much more simple and easy and certain to have one or a few Senators do this on the floor of the Senate than to persuade a state legislature or state convention to oppose the Federal government. The Senator would gain at least some wide notoriety, state officials would have the shadow of a noose hanging over them. Calhoun has been dead more than one hundred years, but his idea, which finally brought the nation to a bloody civil war, still keeps the Congress in a state of helplessness. A few racists can thus protect their empire of hate against the people of a mighty nation.

Over in the House of Representatives, they rely upon a different system because the House does most of its work in committees. Here, they kept the antiquated system of giving committee assignments and chairmanships to members on the basis of length of service. Men from those states which are strongly reactionary on questions of human rights are returned to Congress after Congress, hold chairmanships of committees, and keep bills from being reported out for debate and passage. Congress was helpless for 100 years, therefore, to pass legislation to protect the people of color. In this area of domestic policy it was not a legislative body but a graveyard for human rights. A United States Senator, still as defiant as Calhoun, can say about Civil Rights Bills: "They are all dead because we've got the legislative positions and the power to do something about them. . . . Northern forces have never been able to by-pass our Committee with any bill pertaining to integration."

Think of how much power these people actually have in national party conventions, in Congress, and in the Electoral College. Every man who thinks he would like to be President, and their numbers are great, is almost certain to be careful not to say anything which will offend them. No candidate for nomination is going to stand up and lead any freedom marches. No man can be nominated by either party unless he is a so-called moderate. That means he must be a politician, not a statesman. His statesmanship becomes apparent, if at all, after he is elected. The function of political parties, we are told, is to compromise; to bring together into convention, caucus, and government service, representatives of the people from all sections of a large country; to reconcile their different views and interests in support of a program of public policy; to achieve unity by debate, concession, compromise; in short to serve as the cement of the nation. This may be the function of parties but performance falls far short of profession and is achieved at a terrible sacrifice of progress. Party harmony and solidarity must be maintained even at the expense of the public interest. Parties can not prosper on a diet of internal dissension. Silence and non-performance of duty, therefore, have great appeal. Mediocrity leads to political preferment. The writing of ambiguous platforms develops into an esoteric art. Party discipline and bread and butter expediency both keep the nation in a state of retrogression. This passes under the euphonious name of compromise.

The Whig and Democratic parties were called compromise parties before the Civil War; they were not. The Whig party was a party of silence and inaction. The Democratic party was a party of militant slavery expansion. At the South they did not differ at all on the question of slavery, state rights, and secession, except that the Whigs were reluctant to secede and demanded a show of cause. Southern Whigs and Southern Democrats had tremendous power in their respective parties because of the three-fifths rule and they showed remarkable solidarity in Congress upon all questions touching slavery. They had even greater power in their respective parties after the war and they showed the same solidarity on all questions touching the rights of people of color. This was an explosive issue, likely to break up party solidarity. No President of the United States after Abraham Lincoln until John F. Kennedy, nearly a century later, ever raised the issue in public address. Politicians sold our Constitution and laws for Southern votes. They speculated in the liberties of millions of people. They countenanced anarchy and violence in return for votes. Abraham Lincoln was killed by the hate engendered by rebellion in 1860. John F. Kennedy was just as certainly killed by the hate engendered by rebellion a century later.

The man of color has a right to participate in public affairs at all levels and particularly at the state and local levels. He dare not ever, in any circumstances, agree to less. The same principle holds true in every other area of human rights. Men will always love freedom and equality. They will fight for it because they dare not compromise it away. Justice and right can not be compromised. That is one reason politicians and political parties have shied away from this question as if it were the plague. So the country witnessed a spectacle in the last election never before equalled in American history. The party of Lincoln was pleading for the votes of people in the area of rebellion against Federal authority, assassination of dissenters, and complete subordination of people of color; and, the opposition party was holding a national convention, adopting a platform, and nominating a President without ever calling the roll in order to avoid seating a Negro delegation.

In both cases the people saw an exhibition of the kind of morality that would permit politicians to trade away the rights of the people of color to vote and hold office, and our right as a people to their wisdom in the conduct of public affairs. This was followed by talk of taking representation away from states in proportion as they deny the franchise to people of color, and even more dangerously of Federal legislation to give these people the right to vote in Federal elections. Then some one came up with the idea of Federal registration of voters, but not all of them by any means. Here again there was an attempt at compromise. This amounts to a failure of Congress to deal with the gravest problem facing the nation on even the lowest level. They have done nothing about the filibuster. They have done nothing about the Committee Chairmanship. They have done nothing about elections which should send people of color to either the Senate or House of Representatives from the areas where they live in the greatest numbers.

Excessive political power in Congress, in party conventions, and in the Electoral College gave the white people of the former slave states power to prevent interference of the nation by Congressional legislation in their treatment of people of color. It gave them greater power to do so than they had possessed to protect slavery. It gave them the local autonomy in this respect for which they had rebelled against the Federal government in 1860. It was based upon control of the franchise. Control of the franchise kept people of color out of Congress and out of state and local goverments. It was a clear violation of the United States Constitution. No government which excludes from participation a large portion of the people who pay taxes and are expected to obey the laws, thus violating the principle of consent, is a republican form of government. The Founding Fathers were explicit on that point. James Madison said, "The right of suffrage is certainly one of the fundamental articles of republican government, and ought not to be left to be regulated by the legislature. A gradual abridgment of this right has been the mode in which aristocracies have been built on the ruin of popular forms." Alexander Hamilton was equally emphatic when he said, "A share in the sovereignty of the State, which is exercised by the citizen at large in voting at elections, is one of the most important rights of the subject, and in a Republic ought to stand foremost in the estimation of the law."

Control of the franchise by the states was reinforced by continued state control of the police powers which tolerated, abetted and aided individual and group brutalities unknown in the days of slavery. Congress tried to prevent this by the Thirteenth and Fourteenth Amendments, but the Supreme Court said Congress might not intervene to prevent positive denial of equal protection, or to supplement deficiencies in protection of natural rights of its citizens. It would seem that Congress had always possessed the power to protect persons in their civil rights, if not on the basis of reciprocity of allegiance and protection at least by virtue of the Bill of Rights. In fact, the Constitution itself as the Supreme Law of the land, without Congressional legislation, does so protect. Roger B. Taney said in court in 1819, of the right of free speech, "He must not surrender up the civil and religious rights, secured to him in common with others, by the Constitution of this most favoured nation." It would seem that Congress was empowered to legislate for the protection of persons and property, if not before the Civil War then certainly under the Thirteenth Amendment, because slavery was a comprehensive denial of natural rights and the Amendment abolished slavery. The first Civil Rights Act was passed under the authority of that Amendment. Fearing that an interpretation of that Amendment would not be comprehensive enough, Congress framed the Fourteenth Amendment.

There is widespread ignorance about that clause in the Fourteenth Amendment which says "no state shall make or enforce any law which shall abridge the privileges or immunities of citizens of the United States." The Supreme Court completely changed the language, the meaning, and the purpose of the men who framed the Amendment, when they spoke of "privileges and immunities of United States Citizenship." There is as much difference between the two as there is between day and night. Privileges and immunities was the term used for natural rights and interchangeably used by men fighting for freedom and democracy in this country. The very heart of their philosophy was that natural rights were a gift of the Creator bestowed equally upon all men and enjoyed by all men no matter where they lived or under how many governments they lived. These rights did not derive from man-made laws, nor were they subject to governmental interference. No one knows because no one has ever cared to investigate, how far back in human history men had been looking beyond man-made laws and man-created governments for guidance in their relations with each other and to God. The right to follow, undisturbed and unrestrained by government or by individuals, these several relationships were called the natural rights of man. "Liberty is the right of every human creature as soon as he breathes the vital air; and no human law can deprive him of that right which he derives from the law of nature," said John Wesley. "A slave is a person held as property, by legalized force against natural right," said Salmon P. Chase. "The colonists are by the law of nature free born, as indeed all men are, white or black," said James Otis. "All men have a natural right to be citizens, and to enjoy civil protection in that nation or government where they have a permanent residence, except some legal cause shall prevent it," said James Duncan. These men were talking about the right of every person to be a free moral agent,—a right which involves intelligence, the power to distinguish right from wrong, freedom of conscience and religion, free enquiry and discussion; a right to live under a rule of law and not of man, and to enjoy full equality with every other person in relation to government.

The Fourteenth Amendment forbade any state to abridge such rights of citizens of the United States, and failure to protect—protection being a basic function of government—is assuredly an abridgment, denial, or contradiction. It turned out not to be so. States were held, despite the Amendments, to be the depositaries of individual rights, the national government not to have the power to protect individuals in their rights of persons and property, and privileges and immunities not to mean the natural rights of the individual. The government could not protect its citizens one against another nor punish offenses of one against another. Police powers of the states were left intact.

In reality then, and to all practical purposes, the freedmen were denied the substance of United States citizenship. They continued to live, not in a democracy as free men, but under an oligarchy in a modified form of slavery. We come then to the dreary sequel of abandonment of people of color by the Federal government. St. George Tucker of Virginia declared in 1796 that "Whilst America hath been the land of promise to Europeans, and their descendants, it hath been the vale of death to millions of the sons of Africa." A century later came the haunting beauty of Paul Lawrence Dunbar's lament:

A crust of bread and a corner to sleep in,
A minute to smile and an hour to weep in,

A pint of joy to a peck of trouble,
And never a laugh but the moans come double
And that is life.

A white lawyer and judge speaking with the authority of a professor at William and Mary. A Negro poet and the voice of oppressed millions.

The slaves had managed to survive the whipping posts, the starvation diets, and the cruelties of slavery. They weathered the terrible attrition which the war inflicted upon its innocent victims. They escaped, by God's mercy alone, general slaughter as the fortunes of war turned against their masters. Then, as free men and as citizens of the United States they were beaten down by organized groups of their fellow citizens. The one thing people of color have always had at the hands of white people, in Africa and America, as free men, as slaves, and again as citizens of the United States, is cruelty. We have robbed them of their freedom, of the returns from their labor, of their right to acquire knowledge; but what we have taken away that was by right theirs, pales into insignificance beside the barbarous way in which we have broken and mutilated their bodies and rejoiced in the doing of it.

Two factors are involved in this record of man's inhumanity to man. The man of color, in common with the whole of mankind, loves freedom. He resisted enslavement and he maintained a steady pressure against established authority during the period of enslavement. Freedom gave him the opportunity to become a man once more and that was the one thing the white population would not tolerate. His master had punished him for failure to work or for insolence, or for resistance to his pleasures, or for running away. He had been beaten by other white men at random, by road patrols, and by inspectors, as commanded by law for being abroad without a written permit. He had been shot at random when outlawed and at times of insurrection or rumors of insurrections. The two ever constant factors, however, were (1) corrective action to instill general fear, assure submission, and prevent an assertion of independence; and (2) butchery and devilish cruelty forced upon a people without protection whenever opportunity presented itself to the sadists. People of color were always victims of lust and greed and love of power.

The entire pattern of what was to follow the Civil War was clearly revealed in these events of more than 100 years ago, when statute law and lynch law in the slave states silenced protests against slavery, and lynch law operated against people of color and antislavery whites in the free states. We never have been able to implement Constitutional guarantees in the Black Belt except by Federal force. The Constitution of the United States apparently receives no more respect there from public officials and the people than a scrap of paper.

VI

AN EMPIRE OF HATE

A people fighting for the opportunity to hold slaves forever; who were more concerned about domination by the whites in all aspects of life than about justice; who had hanged slaves indiscriminately on suspicion of intent to revolt; who had surrendered to mob violence anyone suspected of antislavery activities,—such a people could not be expected to abide by the rules of war where people of color were concerned. There were approximately 186,000 of these men in the Union Army, including 145 infantry, seven cavalry and 13 artillery regiments, and 30,000 in the Navy. It is important to remember that they were of four origins: free men from the Northern states, slaves from the conquered areas of the rebellion, fugitive slaves, and slaves from the loyal states who had joined the army with or without the consent of their masters. Louisiana, Kentucky, and Tennesee furnished nearly one-third of the total number.

The free men were citizens of their states and of the United States, and some of them were veterans or sons or grandsons of veterans of the Revolution and War of 1812. The slaves from conquered areas were wards of the government, known as contrabands, under the Confiscation Acts. The fugitive slaves were free after the Emancipation Proclamation. Both contrabands and fugitives were free by military force, therefore by due process of law. If their owners had been killed in armed resistance to the government, that too was by due process of law. These men of color had been caught between the fury of rebellious masters and the solid legions of loyal men. They had died of disease, neglect, and hunger. They had hidden in the canebrakes, the swamps, and the hills, away from the passions of those who sought to drive them back to ruin. They never were safe, they never were free until courageous men like General Hunter on the Sea Islands, and Butler in New Orleans, and Thomas in the lower Mississippi Valley compelled rebels and prejudiced loyalists alike to respect them as men by putting rifles in their hands. Then their own courage put the seal of a great government upon their citizenship.

Let us never forget that the condition of the fugitives who came in a great wave toward the Union army was appalling. If there were nothing else in the way of evidence, the testimony of honorable men on that point would damn the institution of slavery completely. The fugitives were broken in spirit. Some came alone, some brought their families; few had any sort of possessions. Their souls cried out against centuries of oppression. They had been able to see but dimly beyond the limited horizon of the old plantation area. They now came through the heart of a rugged and beautiful timberland; where are the headwaters of rivers that flow to the sea; where men learn the cruelty as well as the beauty of natural law; where they feel the full force and meaning of life and must choose their own destiny. Here they discovered the overpowering majesty of the mountains, the rustle of trees in the ancient forests, the wild animals that roamed in the hinterlands. For the first time, many of them could stand erect and say "I am a man." Their longings increased, their horizons broadened; but their fears deepened with every step they took, for on every mountain path, behind every tree, in every shadow lurked death or cruel retribution. Their only hope was to reach the protection of the Union armies.

The influx forced establishment of refugee camps around the perimeter of the battle area. Grant put the refugees to work harvesting cotton and used the profits to provide food, medical care, and clothing. The army used them as laborers, but it needed help and that help was not slow in coming. Christian benevolence had its roots down deep in America. The men and women of the 1830's, who had dedicated their lives to organized benevolence, had served well both their country and their God. Thousands now entered the portals which had been opened by the army into the vast arena of social reconstruction. Here was confusion and much work to be done, and it was done by the combined efforts of the army and the benevolent societies with the blessing of the civil government.

They went straight to the heart of the problem. There were 3,500,000 men, women, and children, many of them aged, infirm, and sick. They had to be cared for as rapidly as the narrowing limits of the rebellion released them. Their only present source of sustenance was charity, their only hope over the long view was education. So there came into being, in the towns, and on the plantations from which owners or workers or both had fled, training schools for labor and for life, hospitals, and workshops. The purpose was to enrich the nation, spare it the burden of a permanent drain upon charity, and alleviate the disastrous consequences of the rebellion. It was the chaplains, under the inspiring leadership of John Eaton of the Twenty-seventh Ohio Infantry Volunteers in Grant's army, a native of New Hampshire and former superintendent of schools in Toledo, who took over the job of education; and it was the army officers and privates who performed a noble but unrecorded service on a man to man basis.

After 1862 benevolent societies provided the money and the teachers for the schools. The Army furnished subsistence and transportation. The benevolent societies furnished clothing, books and other educational materials. Organizations most active in this work were the American Missionary Society, the New England Freedman's Aid Society of Boston, the Freedman's Relief Association of New York, the Western Sanitary Commission of St. Louis, the Northwest Freedman's Aid Commission of Chicago, and the Western Freedman's Aid Commission of Cincinnati. These organizations had in operation at the close of the war, when the Freedman's Bureau was established by Congress, approximately 1000 schools with 1500 teachers, and 160,000 pupils in schools and orphan asylums.

The work had been accomplished under difficulties almost insurmountable. The white population in the entire area of occupation turned its energies to preventing a solution of the problem instead of helping. Only in Nashville and St. Louis did they contribute to the support of the schools. There were incessant raids by Confederate cavalry, particularly by Wheeler and Forrest, and the farther freedmen were from the army the more difficult it was to maintain schools. Best results were achieved in the West in cities like Vicksburg, Chattanooga, and Memphis, and in the East in the seaports and coastal areas, except for North Carolina. Plantations were isolated. Plantation owners were a law unto themselves. Not much could be done in the way of learning when school hours had to be adjusted to a long day in the cotton field. Teachers were victims of hostility, cruelty, and disease, many dying of yellow fever, smallpox, and plain lack of decent food and living quarters. Both teachers and pupils were abused, subjected to acts of violence, and kidnapped. School buildings were defaced, torn down, and burned.

The attitude of men in rebellion toward all efforts to assist the transition of slaves to freedom and to aid in social reconstruction of the area was no different from their attitude toward people of color in uniform. They used slaves everywhere in their labor battalions. Their war effort was based on slave labor. They used some free persons of color in their enlisted units, but in no case was there any promise of emancipation. They considered all Union men of color as in insurrection for which the penalty was death, and all white officers of these men as guilty of inciting insurrection for which the penalty was death by the laws of all slave states. Governor John Letcher of Virginia demanded from General Jackson the surrender of captured Negro troops and their white officers to be tried under the same law as had been John Brown. General Beauregard wanted to execute all "abolition prisoners" as he called them, by the garrote. Everyone apparently spoke of a Union uniform on a Negro as an "abolition uniform." Secretary of War Seddon said, with regard to the officers: "We ought never to be inconvenienced with such prisoners." This was a general order of Jefferson Davis as early as November, 1862, supported by Act of the Confederate Congress after Lincoln's Emancipation Proclamation. On Christmas Eve, 1862, Davis ordered all Negro prisoners and officers turned over to the states. The Confederate Congress changed the rules and May 1, 1863 ordered Negro troops to be turned over to the states and the officers to be executed after trial by army tribunals. It was not generally enforced because of certain retaliation by the Lincoln Administration. There was substituted for the death penalty a refusal to include soldiers of color in prisoner exchange. This led to a complete breakdown of the exchange system.

More importantly, however, the slaughtering of Negro soldiers instead of taking them prisoners, which had been going on from the beginning of the War, was now intensified. Negro troops were not given the status of prisoners of war. Confederates murdered them at Fort Pillow in Tennessee after they had surrendered. They slipped in behind Burnside's army and killed wagoners. They killed them when Union transports were captured on the Cumberland River. They bayoneted wounded men as they advanced to the attack at Millikens Bend. They murdered prisoners at Poison Spring. God alone knows how many helpless fugitives they murdered in the wake of Sherman's march to the sea. They carried them away into slavery, and they hanged them. Army correspondence makes very clear that the old practice of slave owners was continued of never making a record of punishments or cruelties. It also makes certain that thousands of such cases occurred which can never be documented. That continued after the war and down to the present time. After the second battle of Bull Run, Lee's army was in control of the battlefield, and General Pope was given permission to send men both to bury the Union dead and to care for the wounded. The men were sent on this mission of mercy, but the Negroes who drove the improvised ambulances and dug the graves were seized by the Confederates and sold into slavery. Stonewall Jackson carried away from Harpers Ferry all the Negroes he could lay his hands on. Either Lee knew about it or he was ignorant of what went on in his own army. By January, 1865, he was pleading that slaves be brought into the army as soldiers, and two months later the government heeded his request, but he had never been willing to exchange Negro troops with Grant and one wonders how many such prisoners of war his men actually had taken.

Apparently the choice of murdering or selling into slavery was left pretty much to the soldiers involved. The Richmond *Enquirer* said that, should the Union place Negroes in the field none would be taken prisoner because the troops understood what to do in such cases. It added that if any Negroes had been captured as soldiers in the enemy's ranks the newspaper knew nothing about it. Closely related to this problem is that of why Confederate soldiers who robbed the Union dead of their clothes at night—and by the thousands—and did not hesitate to take the clothing off wounded soldiers on the battlefield, would not rob dead Negro soldiers of their uniforms. There was a specious argument in some Southern newspapers to the effect that Negroes had no right to wear the uniform, and therefore it was not legitimately before the Confederate soldier to be taken. Something of the character of these men is revealed by the behavior of Forrest, who operated with his brothers one of the most infamous slave trading establishments in the country, was brutal in his treatment of Negroes during the war and afterward, yet was said to have had two wives, one white and one black, and two children by each. It is revealed, too, by their turning Union prisoners who were colored or were white citizens of Southern states over to state authorities to be shot as traitors when everyone involved in the rebellion was a traitor to the United States.

Union officers such as Hunter, Butler, Sherman and others were condemned to death in absentia by the Davis government, by state governments, and by field commanders. The practice was almost as common as the earlier one of offering large sums for the delivery dead or alive of prominent anti-slavery leaders. The interesting point is that no matter what the offenses charged against them may have been the broad base of the indictment in every case, as it had been in every charge against anti-slavery men, was incitement of slaves to insurrection. The one thing that saved the captured officers of Negro troops was the large pool of Confederate officers in Union prison camps, and the certainty that 'Rooney' Lee, second son of Robert E. Lee, would be the first one executed in retaliation. General Hunter held the sons of many prominent slave-holders as hostages to make certain that his own men would not be executed if captured. Jefferson Davis's rejoinder to the Emancipation Proclamation, which gave freedom to the slaves, was that it doomed several millions of an inferior race to extermination, and that it incited them to general assassination of their masters by urging them to abstain from violence unless in necessary self-defense. If the English language means anything, here was an open threat of extermination. Who was to do it except Southerners, and where but in the South.

There was more to this, however, than the claim that Union soldiers of color were not engaged in war but in sedition. Davis and his cohorts were claiming a legal, peaceful right of secession. They demanded that it be recognized. They claimed the right of their states to compel citizens of the United States to resist the Federal authority. They denied the right of citizens to obey Federal authority in resistance to state authority. Subordination of the Federal government and subordination of the colored people went together in 1860 and in 1960. The fact that Negro troops had compiled a brilliant record during the war only served to intensify hatred by the Southern whites in defeat. Make no mistake about the contribution of those 165 Regiments. They fought brilliantly in a half-hundred important engagements. Nearly 40,000 of the 186,000 enlisted men lost their lives, and 16 won Congressional Medals of Honor. Make no mistake either of the hatred of Confederate veterans toward them.

It was impossible to keep an army in the South forever, and the killing to beat the Negro down never ceased even momentarily until Congress got control of Reconstruction away from President Johnson. Negroes were killed, raped, and robbed from one end of the South to the other and no record was ever made of individual cases. Then the master terrorist of the slave country, Nathan Bedford Forrest, the commercial slave trader of pre-war days, the murderer of Union prisoners at Fort Pillow, took over and the whole South was honeycombed by organizations of many names but for convenience called the Ku Klux Klan. The Klan has persisted to the present time. It was an organized defiance of all law; a government within a government without legal sanctions; in its origins preaching hatred only of people of color; seeking to destroy every vestige of hope for liberty, justice, and equality; reversing the verdict of the battlefield. Negro citizenship for all practical purposes was transformed over night into a huge joke. Everything they had gained was stripped away. Every brutality ever visited upon their slave parents was revisited upon them. The Klan was organized lawlessness. It was a fountain of hatred. It was the impenetrable barrier to equality. It was to the United States what the Nazis were to Germany. It did not create hatred. It took all of the hatred, violence, and oppression coming out of 200 years of slavery and the rebellion, consolidated it and nourished it through the years. Large parts of the South from that day to this have been under the rule of the Klan. It controls politics, the police, the courts, the schools, the churches, the unions. It represents systematized hatred of the Negro, the Constitution, and the government of the United States.

There is no dividing line between the violence of pre-Klan days and Klan days. The Thirteenth Amendment became a part of the Constitution December 18, 1865, Congress passed a Civil Rights Act over Johnson's veto April 9, 1866. Less than one month later a bloody race riot occurred in Memphis, Tennessee, in which former Confederate soldiers killed 46 Negro refugees and two white men, burned 90 homes, 12 schools, and four churches. In New Orleans, July 30, they killed 35 and wounded 100 more. Schoolhouses were burned in Tullahoma, Shelbyville, Gallatin, Athens, Knoxville, and Columbia. Books and equipment were destroyed with the buildings. The worst of it was that the Negroes were supporting these schools from their meager earnings and there was no way of restoring them. Early the following year, the Ku Klux Klan was organized, and Congress divided the area of rebellion into five military districts under an army of occupation. It was little more than a skeleton force for administrative purposes, having the numerical strength of an ordinary state police force. It gave moral support to the Reconstruction governments but was never strong enough to maintain order against the determined efforts of the Klan. Waves of brutality, murder, and race riots swept across the Black Belt between the years 1868 and 1876 with the worst of the offenses in Louisiana, Tennessee, Mississippi, and South Carolina. New Orleans, Opelousas, Vicksburg, Yazoo City, and Clinton were the scenes of downright massacres. This was a veritable reign of terror with the Klan whipping Negroes; murdering, assaulting, tar-and-feathering schoolteachers; burning the schools, the churches, and the homes where centered the activities which gave faith, knowledge, and self-respect to the newly enfranchised Negroes. It did not arise from poverty of the whites, but from opposition to education for the Negroes, to their participation in public affairs, to their aspiration for equality. Driving out Northern teachers did the job because there were no Southern ones and the school system established by John Eaton was broken up by 1869. Lincoln's hope for a change in the basic structure of Southern life had failed even in the most progressive state, the first to be restored to the Union, in July 1866.

It was perfectly clear even by that time that the Southern people were not going to look upon the Negro any differently after 1865 than they had before unless it be with more scorn and contempt. The concept of racialism was retained, not that of the equality of men. Restraints were removed from the Klan. Schools were segregated. Registration of whites and blacks was kept in separate books. The Federal Civil Rights Act was bitterly denounced and nullified wherever possible. Defeat was inherent in the Reconstruction program because the government had no intention of occupying the South with military forces for a prolonged period.

A horrible wave of brutality, sadism, and anarchy swept over the people of color again as soon as the army was withdrawn and the Reconstruction governments fell. The Federal authorities either could not or would not, but certainly did not, protect them. They were helpless to defend themselves. The state and local governments were apathetic. Even the Civil War did not teach the people of the United States that the rights of men must rest upon something more substantial than prevailing sentiment in a given community; that they must rest upon law and not upon sufferance, upon the national conscience not upon local prejudice. All of the inequities to which the people of color were subjected thereafter added up to an imperfect freedom derived from the will of the community and dependent upon toleration rather than right.

The history of the pre-war antislavery contest,

of the war itself, and of the post-war strife in the former slave states shows that, where local government controls the affairs of men, the rights of men depend not upon the spirit of the law but upon the caprice of their fellow men at any given time and that is precarious tenure indeed. The idea that the degree of civil freedom belonging to any person can rightfully be fixed by popular sentiment is wrong. Local government will not protect in the case of minority groups or of persons it dislikes, or regards as inferior, or fears. These are the people who most need the protection of law because they ordinarily do not have the wealth, the education, the family connections, or any of the other intangible assets which safeguard the rights of so many against encroachment. These were the freedmen at the close of the Civil War. State laws went right on allowing the white people to do what they had always done. Victims were only people of color and life was cheap. The will of the community, reinforced by the heavy hand of death, denied them equality of public services and enjoyment of the amenities of life, restricted their earning capacity, controlled their lives by irresponsible private power and arbitrary police authority, and permitted education for work only and that in moderation. They continued to live in squalid shacks because they were not allowed to live elsewhere. They were denied access to work commensurate with their ability, being excluded from all but unskilled labor in the white man's economic world. They served in our wars and came back to squalor and oppression. They accepted it or starved or got out. They were victims of economic discrimination, political exclusion, social rejection, and inferior education. It was not and is not a question of civil rights. It was unfinished business. It was the survival of slavery in a land dedicated to freedom, a colossal betrayal of the principles on which the nation was founded, a continuation of the age-long struggle of men to be free, of human rights versus slavery for control of the nation, of democracy in all its radiance against privilege and arbitrary power.

The nation shrank from its full responsibility in 1787 and paid for its error with the lives of 300,000 young men. It did the same in 1867 and ushered in a century of paganism turned to anarchy. The people of color had to be beaten down and they were beaten, hanged, burned, mutilated, and otherwise tortured. This was the era of lynchings—the same old formula—the same old method—the same old objective—both on a grand scale and in a manner to attract the attention of the civilized world. These lynchings were ofttimes great public attractions, advertised in advance and attended by thousands of people. Between 1900 and 1930, there were 302 in Georgia, 285 in Mississippi, 201 in Texas, 172 in Louisiana, 170 in Florida, 132 in Alabama, and lesser numbers in other states to a total of 3,714. This was anarchy, a complete desecration of constitutional government. It was government by men and not by law. These mobs claimed to represent the will of their communities. They had claimed as much both North and South before the War when they roamed the streets of the cities spreading death and destruction, and we suppose in a sense they did because it is difficult to say who is most guilty, the ignorant and depraved who perpetrate such crimes or those who know the enormity of the offenses but do nothing to prevent them. Every person who ever committed an act of violence on a person of color is known or could have been known to law enforcement agencies.

A high percentage of those lynched, both men and women, were innocent of all wrong. The objective was to beat the people of color down by fear. Many were lynched for such offenses as trying to act like a white man, seeking employment, acting as strike-breakers, using offensive language, making boastful remarks. Many of the victims were framed, by women for instance to cover their own indiscretions. Lynchings, like the trials of slaves in earlier days, quickly prevented any evidence being established, any testimony being presented, any possibility of acquittal. The basis of mob action was always rumor and the death of the victim the only certain fact.

Victims, as of old, were hunted with bloodhounds. There was always an eagerness for the hunt that could produce a mob in a matter of minutes and a craving for the satisfaction of momentary power shown by mock trials and executions. For one moment in their lives a few men could play God, sheriff, judge, jury, and executioner. They would have chased their victims to Hell and back if necessary for that and they did take them from officers of the law, from jails, from court rooms, and from hospital beds. Mobs were frequently more interested in torture than in the killing itself. Victims were sometimes tied to trees or fence posts and used for target practice. Their toes and fingers were cut off one joint at a time. Their teeth were pulled out with pliers. Their testicles were crushed, or cut off, or burned off. They were strangled. They were roasted over slow fires. Their bodies, after they were dead, were soaked with gasoline and burned. They were dragged by ropes behind trucks until the flesh was torn from their bodies. Women, sometimes with babies in their arms, and children went to these affairs. Mothers were known to have wakened their children to take them to lynchings. Thousands of people were involved. Law enforcement officials bowed to the will of these mobs and seldom would juries indict or convict.

The reasons for this Roman orgy are not hard to find. The Africans were captured, torn from their homeland, and made beasts of burden in a distant land. They were freed, with a great deal of help from themselves, given citizenship in the land of their humiliation, and suffered from the gift of the ballot at the hands of their country as much as they had from the gift of their color at the hands of God. More of them were shot down in the first twenty years of freedom than in 200 years of slavery. Every step forward in knowledge and self-respect hardened resistance. All they ever wanted and asked for was an equal chance in the race of life, a chance to be men. It is a great tragedy that social reconstruction could not have been achieved in a respectable manner, but the white people were drunk with power, frenzied by the thought of interference, and confirmed in the practice of evil deeds and doctrines for nearly a century. That is a matter of history. They would not have any part of it. Lawlessness in the former rebellious area to prevent it was appalling and to a large degree successful. Civil and political rights are still denied the people of color after a century of citizenship. This concept of a white man's government grew stronger through the years. The man of color who aspired to cast a ballot was dangerous, he must be driven out or shot unless he renounced his rights as a man and a citizen. We do not know how much weight to give to each of the several causes of this behavior but know with certainty what is involved and it is neither pleasant nor good from any point of view.

The first is a determination to keep an outmoded, undemocratic, even vicious political system which gives to the dominant whites complete control of local governments, tremendous influence in political parties, and the power to keep Congress from passing laws for the benefit or protection of the people of color. It gives white men in the old slave states, with the lowest cultural level in the nation, a great deal more power than anyone else in government. They had it because they were slaveholders. They have it because they oppress people of color and keep them from voting. Hatred has smothered the law. It is the controlling factor. The white people did not intend that the freedmen ever should make decisions or participate in public affairs, not if they had to go to the brink of racial war to prevent it.

The second cause of oppression is a measure of personal happiness. Inequality seems at times to be nearer people's hearts than liberty itself. There are millions who walk away from those who weep, from those who are bowed down by heavy burdens, from those who are lost in the storm and have nowhere to turn because they are despised. They measure their happiness by someone else's misery, their riches by someone else's poverty, their intelligence by someone else's ignorance. It seems paradoxical that such a large part of our personal satisfaction comes not from the richness of our own spiritual and material possessions but from the poverty of our neighbors.

Not more than one-third of the white population of the slave states had any direct connection with slavery. It kept the slave states poor. It put a stigma upon labor. It prevented the establishment of schools. It drove the poor man out or up into the back country. But the non-slaveholding population did nothing about it and one of the reasons was because they could look about them and see this large population of slaves so infinitely worse off than themselves. The same held true after the Civil War. So long as they could keep the Negro down, they were content, actually smug about their own ignorance, poverty, low level of culture, and second rate achievements. So the interests of the genteel politician and the 'red-neck' were joined. People of color must never be allowed to make decisions or enter into the competition of achievement. The white man had found his artificial badge of superiority in the paleness of his skin. It was not man against man but one portion of the population against another. The degree to which people of color insisted upon equality before the law was the measure of the degree of violence upon them. Trouble did not come from a recognition of equal rights but from their denial.

The third cause of oppression had to do with sex. One can not dig very deep into the history of slavery or into the post-war era of race relations without being aware of its importance. Female slaves were fair game for any white man. Thousands were bought and sold for no other purpose and every place of public accommodation had its complement of female slaves to wait upon gentlemen guests. Slaveholders, their sons, overseers, and apparently anyone else of mercurial temperament had a field day. There was no one to whom the woman could appeal for protection without danger of terrible punishment. The law provided no protection. Slaves were only property and rape was trespass. The enormous amount of mixed blood forced back into the slave population was proof of their helplessness. It was one of the reasons, and a very powerful one, for the fight to preserve slavery. One very competent authority says that fifty per cent of the people of color in the Southern cities in 1860 were of mixed blood.

The situation was no different after the war.

The grievances of these oppressed people were many, and they are sickening, but the one expressed with most vehemence and bitterness even today is the inabilty of the men to protect their women. They were vulnerable to abuse by employers, landlords, and professional men of every sort. Complaint led only to heartaches at home, resistance led to starvation, and reprisal led to death. It was the price an oppressed people had to pay for the poor privilege of staying alive. White women hated the victims of their menfolk, and it was the white women who would not accept association of the two groups except upon the basis of their own superiority. Equality was ruled out.

In the fourth place, people are cruel and happily so. They are more cruel to their fellow men than they are to animals. The whites were unspeakably cruel to the slaves and they were equally so to the freedmen. Their victims had a will to resist which fed the flames of passion. Slaves were whipped and branded and castrated and starved by their owners and overseers whose will was law. Pregnant women were hunted with dogs, and slaves who ran away were shot. Freedmen were whipped and castrated and hanged and burned and shot and set upon by dogs. There was no one to protect them as slaves and there was no one to protect them as free persons. Why should a people who had learned to love brutal exhibitions give up its ready made pool of victims about whom no one was concerned.

Finally, there was the refusal of the old slave states to accept the verdict of the Civil War. The

South always had been a land of stagnation and frustration and the Negro was blamed for the whole of it. The Union was dedicated to freedom but the South was determined to keep slaves. The Union, like the rest of the civilized world, was moving toward freedom and equality for all men but the South chose to break up the Union to preserve slavery. It lost the war because its constitutional philosophy of decentralization could destroy but not create a nation. It clung to the doctrine and to as much of slavery as it could salvage because it was the key to white supremacy. The central theme of Southern history is Negro inferiority.

When historians continued to talk about slavery as a humane and benevolent institution, and anthropologists about racial inequalities as an established scientific fact; when the flag of rebellion was flown beside or above the Stars and Stripes in schoolrooms; when men in public office shouted from the housetops their devotion to state sovereignty which never was; when preachers, and teachers, and lawyers, and newspaper editors demanded segregation forever,—when all these things were true, and the Ku Klux Klan was allowed to flourish, is there any wonder that people of color were beaten and shot and treated like dogs. So were a people crucified. Three centuries of oppression! Three centuries of patient effort to attain full measure of freedom! Emancipation was something more than a formality. It carried with it the common rights of men. We failed to sustain those rights and freedom became a mockery.

ENSLAVED

Oh when I think of my long suffering race,
For weary centuries despised, oppressed,
Enslaved and lynched, denied a human place
In the great life line of the Christian West;
And in the Black Land disinherited,
Robbed in the ancient country of its birth,
My heart grows sick with hate, becomes as lead,
For this my race that has no home on earth.
Then from the dark depths of my soul I cry
To the avenging angel to consume
The white man's world of wonders utterly;
Let it be swallowed up in earth's vast womb,
Or upward roll as sacrificial smoke
To liberate my people from its yoke!

Claude McKay

We pass then to a pattern of oppression much broader in scope. Segregation was renewed in all of its hateful forms, some of which prevailed throughout the entire nation and grew worse through the years. The person of color might have refuse scattered in his yard, crosses burned before his home, stones thrown through his window. He might be shoved off the streets, or abducted at night and severely beaten, or have his house burned down. He might be discharged from his job. The bus might pass him by as he waited in vain for public transportation. Hospitals might refuse him admittance. Physicians and dentists might be always too busy to serve his needs. Banks might refuse him credit. His neighbors might set up elaborate schemes to prevent him from buying or renting property in the community. He might sit unserved in a public restaurant, wait for hours to buy a pair of shoes, or be tossed bodily out of a bar. All of these things might happen and have happened a million times because the protection of persons and property is in the hands of local police officials. They can be and are negligent in performance of their duty and brutal in their treatment of individuals who have done no wrong, and they were invariably both where the person of color was concerned. What could these people do when police officials would not protect and juries would not convict. Officials behaved like people wanted them to behave or they were not elected to office. White people were protected against police brutality and illegal arrest because they were white people. The people of color had no protection at all except the law, and there was no one to make police officials obey the law. They sat behind shuttered windows at night; and none of them ever walked down a street with complete assurance of being able to get home again unmolested.

Prejudice, discrimination, oppression,—call it what you will—against our people of color is a form of social insanity. It is destroying all of us. Whatever harms a part of society harms all of it. It is destroying our government. God himself gave color to man and from that color we have fashioned a single law that supersedes all constitutions and statutes: the law of public opinion in a community. It destroys equality. When some people have to obey the orders of other people equality is extinguished.

"The sure guaranty of peace and security of each race," said Justice John Marshall Harlan, "is the clear distinct, unconditional recognition by our governments, national and state, of every right that inheres in civil freedom, and of equality before the law of all citizens of the United States without regard to race. . . . We boast of freedom enjoyed by our people above all other people. But it is difficult to reconcile that boast with a state of law which, practically, puts the brand of servitude and degradation upon a large class of our fellow citizens, our equals before the law." John Marshall Harlan had been a slaveholder. He had been opposed to the Thirteenth Amendment. But he had fought under Thomas to preserve the Union and Constitutional government. He believed in justice, in equality of rights, and in government by law.

VII

NEW HORIZONS

Subordination of people of color in the United States is a gross violation of the most precious rights of men, utterly inconsistent with morality, and totally irreconcilable with the spirit and principles of our national existence. If the politicians, the educators, the lawyers, the preachers would raise their voices against this enormous evil, it might soon be eradicated. The old order is gone. This is revolution. Our society must be set free from the restraints of a mouldering past. There is no possibility of standing still. We must go forward or backward. We must go forward or the rest of the world will pass us by. There is no half way, no middle way, no other way. We must give to every person his personal security and his Constitutional rights. We must regain our faith in the basic principles of democracy and we must keep the faith. Those principles are irresistible. They will live as long as man survives. If the country must be destroyed by pagans, let the evil come from without, not from within, for then we shall rise again. We must do today what it will be too late to do tomorrow. Yet, every time we try to do anything, we are up against impregnable barriers.

There seems to be no limit to the variety of intimidation and actual violence in the old Black Belt. There is racial war in a very real sense. It could quickly merge into civil war and then into world war. Parents, children, criminal elements, public officials, police, and the courts are all involved in one way or another. Parents picket, throw rocks, hurl epithets, spit upon children. Some children hurt other children in brutal fashion, and use violent language which can only be an echo of what they have heard at home. Police ofttimes can think only of suppression, and treat children like criminals, and both people of color and their friends with shameful disregard for civil rights. Criminal elements, secret orders, and sometimes Citizens Councils and governors incite to riot and resort to bombings, beatings and outright murder. Authorities of public schools, colleges, and universities are under tremendous pressures. Every effort is made to shift the blame for what happens upon someone else, and also the responsibiliy for doing something about it. The Federal government gets most of the blame, the school officials most of the responsibility, and the children most of the suffering.

God alone knows the heartaches and sorrow and mortification of parents who must explain to little children every day that they can not drink from this or that water fountain, nor buy in this or that store, nor go to this or that school; that there are places they can not go because the color of their skin will pollute the whole area.

Poor little boys and girls, innocent of all wrong,
Compelled to go and sit in other schools alone,
Because they might excel in competition,

Cursed be the people who hurt a little child
To please the ignorant, stupid fools among them;
Whose only joy in life derives from feeling smug,
Self-satisfied, content to live in ignorance,
Poverty, misery, if some one else appears
To be worse off than they, however handicapped
By unjust prejudice.

This madness destroys the one everlasting miracle: that of motherhood. Jesus said: "Suffer little children to come unto me, for of such is the kingdom of heaven." The slaveholders commanded female slaves to go and breed, for children were gold and luxury and ease.

The female slave was wife and mother, concubine,
Prey of all who feared not owner's wrath, or
conscience,
Bearing child, driven to the fields without respite,
Enduring child-birth pains with deep humiliation,
Knowing not the father of the child she suckled,
Feeling not the comfort or hope of motherhood.
Her child would be a slave for life, never a man;
Beaten down to the earth, humble, lowly, listless,
Meanly looked upon, meanly treated by all men
His equals before God.

Today we do not sell them, we set dogs on them, drive them from our libraries, throw them into jail for trying to buy a sandwich, bomb them in the House of God. In this area of human relationships as nowhere else, the racists have sold their souls to keep the colored man down in the ditch. So long as he is there, he is living proof of inferiority. They fail to see how far down they themselves must go and have gone to keep him there. They are never free from a haunting fear of retribution. Fear makes them cruel; cruelty becomes an obsession that leads to madness. Unable to justify their acts by reason, they can no longer distinguish between right and wrong.

Indifference to the situation in other parts of the country is depressing. Grandchildren of men who died to free the slaves now sympathize with the oppressors. The foul spirit of tyranny still emanates from the graveyard of slavery to spread contempt for men of color throughout the land. The situation continues because people who ought to know better permit it to continue. Whether the silence of many editors, preachers, business men, and professional men is due to bread and butter expediency, to cowardice, to blunted moral sensibility, or to plain indifference is not readily apparent. All of them know that people of color are despoiled of their civil and political rights. People read newspapers more than they read the Bible and they can not help but know, but it is precisely the informed who do not speak.

All kinds of people in all kinds of ways have tried to do something about racialism, and all have failed because too many want compromise and human rights can not be compromised. They have failed, also, because efforts have been piecemeal and this is a matter of all or nothing. It is so simple division is impossible. They failed because people think, if they think at all, that the problem will gradually disappear. Truth and morality no longer seem to have an appeal. Perhaps they never did have, perhaps we have read history backward. The mass of the people are not interested because it is not their own personal problem. They have not, as individuals, committed an offense against anyone. They see no cause for excitement. They do not know. It is not easy to get people interested in truth. One may write a whole shelf-full of philosophical treatises and never create a whisper of reform. There has to be a great and apparent corruption of some popular institution to arouse the people. Racialism has done more. It has corrupted our government, our churches, our schools, our very souls. It has destroyed our humanity and our common sense. We have gone on for generations priding ourselves on our democracy without realizing how emaciated it really has become. We are more disturbed today about smoking cigarettes than we are about discrimination. One destroys the body, the other kills the soul. Physical suicide, though it be slow and painless, disturbs us, moral suicide not at all.

Our children can not bring their little Negro friends home to play. Their parents are not welcome at our dinner parties. We bar them from the ballot box. We will not sit beside them at the theatre. They can not kneel beside us at the communion table. They can not buy or rent a home in our neighborhood. They can not eat in our restaurants, or sleep in our motels, or sit down in our toilets. They are exploited by day and by night, by the landlords and by merchants, and by the lords of the underworld, and there isn't much difference in the end result. We keep them poor and do our best to keep them ignorant. They are arrested and searched and beaten and annoyed interminably by police. They are forced to take the end of the line whether it be for the sacraments or jobs or public accommodations. They pay and pay and pay in money and heartaches and tears for things that are theirs by right, and millions of white people in the country are guilty at some time or other of a sneer or a stare or a cold shoulder which can be more cruel than a knife blade.

So long as the man of color must daily drink a cup of bitterness, so long as his presence is looked upon as an evil, he can not hope to realize the normal aspirations of the human heart. His freedom of choice in professions and other walks of life is greatly restricted. He is handicapped in the large universities, in graduate and professional schools, because his education has been in schools of inferior quality. When he overcomes all of these handicaps, he finds great difficulty in getting established in work commensurate with his skills, and even more in securing promotions. Men of color have long been excluded from the faculties of many colleges, from fellowships for graduate and professional study, and even from enrollment as undergraduate students.

The city mayor, the chief of police, the councilman, the state legislator, the governor, the Congressman all spend a lot of time, energy, and money getting elected. They are politicians. Their jobs are their bread and butter. They keep their political fences in repair and rarely if ever do anything unless it is what the people want. They bow to prejudice. They move with the cunning of cats to avoid offense to the prejudices of their constituents. They pull and back and twist and turn themselves inside out. They practice the arts of evasion and equivocation and ambiguity. They shift responsibilities to the courts. They help each other in party conventions. There must be harmony in the party though there be bedlam in the House of God and revolution in the land.

Real estate agents are not going to offend home owners. City managers and mayors are not going to offend real estate agents or home owners. Bankers are not going to risk their money in loans to people who already have three strikes against them in the savage world of economic competition. The person of color is in that situation because he is the last one hired and the first one fired, is excluded from many types of employment, and is the inevitable victim of everybody who robs and cheats and plunders the poor. School superintendents are not going to risk their jobs by hiring people of color as teachers. Dentists, doctors, barbers, hotel managers, restaurant owners, merchants are not going to lose white patrons in order to serve people of color. Some of them are slaves to their passions and prejudices, some are too cowardly to resist pressures, and some are satisfied to take the easy way. How they live with themselves; what they tell their children; what they are going to tell their God; these remain the secrets most will carry to their graves.

Racialism finds its greatest anchorage in institutions and sooner or later every human interest becomes institutionalized. A cursory list would include such organizations as churches, fraternal orders, labor unions, associations of scholars and professional men, bankers, and farmers; service clubs; cooperatives; country clubs; sororities; women's clubs; and a multitude of others. All such organizations are for fellowship or solidarity in protection, and every one of them in some form or other forges chains to bind us and prevent complete freedom of action, and every one of them is under tremendous pressure to promote uniformity, exclusiveness, and harmony. They were white in origin, they are to large degree white now, and they may well remain white to the end of time. Where is the answer? In the church, in the schools, in the government, and in the hearts of men.

It has required remarkable courage to stand up to the buffeting the people of color have taken. The glory is that they no longer are dejected, and despondent, and constrained to give up the struggle. It may come to pass that they shall lead the way to a regeneration and a revitalization of our democracy. They began this reformation, and they may well have to finish it; but this nation can never afford to allow the reformation to cease. If the man of color does not carry it forward, we must, in fulfillment of our obligations to God and a more abundant life for all mankind.

The church is the one agency whose primary responsibility is reformation, both of individuals and society. It is the duty and high privilege of churchmen to condemn evil, corruption, and despotism in government. It is their duty to castigate immoral conduct on the part of individuals. The trouble is we have fallen into two major errors in this country. The first is that the church must never interfere with government. The church said slavery was a Christian institution and a political question. Preachers owned slaves, church organizations owned slaves and so far as possible criticism of slavery was suppressed in pulpits, conferences, and church publications in conformity with the idea of separation of state and church. Slavery was held to be a political not a moral question. If it were a sin, it pertained to society, was sanctioned by civil authority, and was not a matter of individual accountability. We are dealing here with survival of slavery as a system, and hundreds of thousands of people take that position today in regard to laws which deprive people of color of equality.

The church is something more than a place for psalm singing and long prayers, and this is something more than a question of politics, economics, and law. Any person who subscribes to the Judeo-Christian faith, who thinks he can have his professed faith and hate, prejudice, racialism at the same time is a fool. It is the duty of churchmen to tell him so. In all the world there is one haven of refuge—one sanctuary—which towers above all others where the helpless, the destitute, the oppressed may find anchorage, and that is the church. Churchmen have the high duty and responsibility to speak in defense of weak, exploited, helpless people; to condemn unjust laws and courts; even as it is the duty of every citizen to maintain the highest standard of morality in relation to his government, at the ballot-box, in legislative bodies, in court rooms, and in executive offices. The responsibilities of churchmen and of laymen in this respect are inseparable. In all of history, the great leaders of men, able and willing to denounce tyranny, to condemn evil, to arouse the people in time of crisis and lead them in the paths of peace, have been the priests, the preachers, and the prophets.

Precious are the days of youth, when our hearts have no wounds, our minds no prejudices, our souls no remorse. Then, if ever, justice, equality, and peace find fertile soil. Then, if ever, is the future of our institutions and the safety of our country made secure; yet, it is precisely at this point that democracy has failed miserably. We all know that education must be universal; that if we miss one child we may lose for all time an Einstein. We know there must be no enforced segregation because that is totally incompatible with equality of men and the democratic philosophy of human right. We know the light must flow through unobstructed; the search for the truth, and the truth freely and fully spoken separate education from indoctrination. We know that the purpose of education is to enrich the lives of men and women, to train their reasoning powers, to improve their skills and productive ability, to give them greater earning capacity. Where then have we failed? In the sense that education is, also, and primarily, for the enrichment of our social environment: to train our public servants, our lawyers, our doctors, our dentists, our nurses, our research scholars, our teachers and preachers, our journalists.

Every one of these people has a vital part to play in society. We train them in our schools. The poorest among us pays taxes to make their education possible. We confer degrees upon them. In so doing, we say to the world that they have proved their ability to meet the standard of work required for the degree. If that were all that education meant, we had better lock up the whole establishment. It means a degree of achievement in character and intelligent citizenship. It means, hopefully, that deep in their minds and hearts are ideas that will enrich the growth of civilization. It means they have been prepared to become a part of that never ending stream of culture flowing from a distant past on into an endless future. It means a stamp of approval has been placed upon them as qualified members of a college community, a school faculty, a hospital staff, a local government, a national defense agency. It means they are honorable men and women, intelligent citizens, and that they are not going out to prostitute their talents and their skills to selfish purposes or special interests. They are going to heal the minds and bodies of the infirm, protect the weak, serve their fellow men, and do everything within their power to promote happiness, harmony and peace in their communities and throughout the world.

An educated man seeks to probe the deeper mysteries of life and add to our store of accumulated knowledge. He tries to enrich his own life and give it meaning. He hopes above everything else to learn how better to serve his fellow men. No one must be neglected in the process of education. No one must be neglected in the service we give. Here is the dignity of man in all its splendor. Free to enter into friendly competition with his fellow men. Equipped to do so. Dedicated to serving his fellow men as their needs may require. Associating with his fellow men according to the amenities of life. Accepting as graciously of their help as he has given generously of his own. Making his contribution to that great reservoir of moral and intellectual power that is the strength of the nation.

Our failure in government is even more pronounced than in religion and education. There is something startling about the defiance of Federal authority by state and local units of government today, one hundred years after the Civil War. *Something startling! Something tragic!* Startling because those governors who fly the flag of rebellion and set themselves up as sacred symbols of Americanism live and dream in a world of fantasy. The world of reality has passed them by forever. Tragic because they are heroes and prophets to many people. They probably could be elected and reelected as long as they live. They demand segregation forever, shout defiance at the Federal government, mock at the national conscience, and curse the Federal courts.

There is something awe-inspiring, something very comforting about the dignity of the Supreme Court. Here is the law in all its majesty and the wisdom of generations of people combined and applied to the protection of one man's lesser rights, against abuse by some person or some arbitrary authority. The Supreme Court is not God; its judgments are of this world; but in the Court is the greatest security of every individual person. Yet, despite this fact, the Court has been vilified by politicians not worthy to serve as page boys in its sacred precincts.

State and local authorities have taken us back 1000 years with their arrests for trespass. They have treated citizens of the United States with the utmost brutality. They have defied every agency of the Federal government, sneered at every constitutional provision for the protection of individual rights; and they have done it successfully. This abuse of governmental power by secondary authorities in the nation derives from state and local control by men who are prepared to use every form of intimidation, even to the point of murder against anyone who opposes them, and because their victims have no voice at the ballot box. The most terrifying exercise of their power is their desecration of the jury system. Indictment, trial, and conviction or acquittal by one's peers has long been regarded as sacred. What good is it when one's peers, so called, hate him because of the color of his skin, and are as ready to lynch him in the court room as in the cotton field?

Everyone knows the racists have control in large areas of the country, and in those areas a white man can shoot a person of color, or burn his house, or help to mutilate him without fear of indictment by a jury. The country has allowed itself to be intimidated by these people where it is unwilling to enforce the right of people of color to the franchise. This is not alone a question of right. No nation can afford to be deprived of the wisdom and counsel of millions of its people in the conduct of its government either on local, state, or national level. Its guarantee to all is the first step in reconstruction. If we are going to restore harmony, erase the scars of generations of oppression, and insure peace among ourselves, we must start at the polls and in the court room. Thousands of people each year are called to jury service. It is one of our most solemn obligations; not to be taken lightly; and not to be evaded. Every man's rights, even life, may depend upon proper functioning of the jury system at any time. Destroy it and tyranny is inevitable. Those who invade Constitutional and inalienable rights of men by perversion of judicial processes—those who sit upon juries only to disregard justice and right—are guilty of fearful perjury. Violation of the law by those who are sworn to uphold it is fatal to liberty.

This is no longer a matter of state and local business. It is the business of the people of the United States. Schools and libraries and welfare agencies, and licensing of professional men, and police protection, and a host of other functions of government are everybody's business when people roam all over the country by millions to live; and so it is their business to demand that every person have something to say about making the laws under which he lives. We have got to demand that every law enforcement agency of the Federal government be charged with the responsibility of protecting the persons and property of citizens of the United States, and of apprehending and punishing offenders. If it is necessary to have an Amendment to the Constitution for this purpose, then let us get on with the business. It does not seem possible that state and local governments in large areas of the country ever will protect people of color. Very few offenses by individuals and law enforcement officers ever are recorded. Less often are offenders brought to trial and punished. This can not go on because we stand on the verge of civil strife today.

What did Benjamin Franklin say about this? "That every man of the community except infants, insane persons, and criminals, is of common right, and by the laws of God, a freeman and entitled to the free enjoyment of liberty. That liberty or freedom consists in having an actual share in the appointment of those who frame the laws, and who are to be the guardians of every man's life, property, and peace; for the all of one man is as dear to him as the all of another; and the poor man has an equal right, more need to have representatives in the Legislature than the rich one.

"That they who have no voice nor vote in the election of representatives do not enjoy liberty; but are absolutely enslaved to those who have votes and to their representatives; for to be enslaved is to have governors whom other men have set over us, and to be subject to laws made by the representatives of others, without having had representatives of our own to give consent in our behalf."

Nobody may expect regeneration in local government where it is most needed. Racists are adamant. They are familiar with all of the tricks and evasions. They are not going to confer the right of suffrage, for example, without distinction of color. They should not have the power to confer or withhold. Hope lies in national authority and only national authority. The Federal government has power—it needs disposition. Slaveholders never had any difficulty in finding power in the Constitution to do what they wanted to do in the way of oppression. Why should we find any difficulty in finding the power to protect innocent people. State rights carried to their inevitable conclusion brought war and war brought freedom to the slave. It behooves every man to ponder well that simple historical fact. Violence reminiscent of the 1850's is building up again. Should it continue, it will be met by violence and every vestige of discrimination against people of color will be swept away; but with it will go every important power of the state governments.

People of color are moving ever more rapidly to urban centers. Already the cities are more powerful than states. They are not going to be controlled by the states forever, and in those cities the people of color whose history bears nothing but oppression, bitterness, and misery at the hands of state governments will have a controlling voice. Everything these people ever have they will owe to themselves, and as far as governments are concerned to the United States government. The very nature of the problem which faces us compels closer relationships between national and city governments. State governments may well be found to have outlived their usefulness.

The dignity of man and the equality of all men in the sight of God are inescapable facts of eternal life. The equality of all men under the law and in the administration of justice, also, lest we forget, is the foundation of liberty. Its continued denial will hasten the decline of civilization in America. The one great political crime in this country is the cruel tyranny with which the people of color have been treated, and that is one of the undeniable facts of our history.

There wasn't much the slaves could do but pray, and pray they did, in their lonely cabins, in the cotton fields, and by the auction block, by day and by night, laboring under the threat of the driver's whip or fleeing from the pursuer's bloodhounds. Freedom gave them a little more elbow room, but not much. They had run away from slavery, now they ran away from lynching. They went to the cities and were caught in race riots. They went to the courts and ended up in chain gangs. They suffered every day of their lives for generations, and always at the hands of professed Christians; but they refused to lose their manhood. They taught their children never to be satisfied with anything less than the treatment which is the right of a man and a citizen. They taught them at home and at school never to efface themselves because of their color.

It was a constant struggle, a long struggle, because of centuries of oppression and continued resistance. It is not easy to fight the law and one's neighbors too, if one wants to live, not when one is poor, perhaps uneducated, not ever. Many times young people have told me of days when they wanted to shut themselves away from a white man's world, weary from the constant battle against compromise with evil; but they have come too far now for self-effacement. Some months ago I was sitting in the moot court room of a leading Negro college of an old slave state, momentarily discussing with faculty and students the greatest crime of the twentieth century, assassination of the second President involved in this contest for the survival of civilization in America. In answer to a question from a brilliant, courageous, and lovely young lady who had been beaten and jailed many times by the racist power structure of local governments, I said there would be no solution to our problem until Christians started behaving like Christians; to which she replied: "I don't know what you are talking about, there are no Christians." Finally, she said: "I do not know what the next step shall be, [she had been talking about self-immolation] but I shall continue to fight until every man in America is free, even if it means giving my life." Later, she quoted those famous lines of Claude McKay:

If we must die, let it not be like hogs
Hunted and penned in an inglorious spot,
While round us bark the mad and hungry dogs,
Making their mock at our accursed lot.
If we must die, O let us nobly die,
So that our precious blood may not be shed
In vain; then even the monsters we defy
Shall be constrained to honor us though dead!

Here was despair! Here was the spirit of self sacrifice! Here was Gabriel, and Denmark Vesey, and Nat Turner all over again. Here was Joan of Arc. Here was 1919—human rights or death. The dignity of man or blood in the streets. Revolution? Civil War? No one knows—too few care. Negroes had prayed as slaves and as free men. They had prayed for mercy and for understanding. They had been segregated in the turmoil of life, in the worship of God, and in the silence of the grave. The church had failed them. The fairest government on earth had failed them. They had no place to turn, so they stopped turning, stopped running, stopped looking anywhere but to their own strength and courage for salvation. Their experiences have given them a depth of spiritual power unknown to the whites today. They have achieved and maintained a nobility of character that puts them in a remarkably strong position in the present contest for recognized equality.

Woodrow Wilson once said: "The thoughts of plain people here and everywhere throughout the world, the people who enjoy no privileges and have simple and unsophisticated standards of right and wrong, is the air all governments must henceforth breathe if they would live." National authority in the area of human rights is so feeble in the United States as to be almost non-existent. Yet, a little while as the lives of nations go and even as a nation we shall not have complete freedom in these matters. Nations the world over are pledged collectively to promote "respect for human rights and for fundamental freedoms for all without distinction as to race, sex, language, or religion." Indifference throughout the world to our behavior is gone. If this challenge of racialism is to be met, it must be met now. If it is to be settled, it must be by this generation. It will be a peaceable settlement or no settlement at all, and probably no further need for one.

The greatest revolution in the history of man in the area of human relationships is moving with tremendous force. It has purpose and leadership. It will release the spirits, the minds, the creative abilities of millions from thralldom. No one can see the end. Anyone who thinks what is happening in this country is a little family quarrel is doomed to a sad awakening. There will be indiscretions, excesses, confusion, indifference, neutrality, humiliation. There will be tremendous tension at times, but the fight for freedom and justice will go on, even at the fearful risk of civil strife. Men can not turn back in their quest for a better life even in election years. We have somehow to find the courage, the ability, and the faith to keep abreast. Our cultural heritage goes back many centuries through Western Europe to the Mediterranean world of Greece and Rome. Our language, literature, law, and political institutions have come down to us largely through England, with some modifications by adjustments to our needs as a pioneering people. On any account, it is the culture of the white Christian Western World that predominates; but we do have in our population 20 million people whose direct cultural heritage, and instinctive devotion, largely go back to the vast continent of Africa.

What should have been our proudest asset became our shame. Every time I turn around I bump into someone who says that if we accord equal rights and privileges to people of color, we will have Negro and white equality, and pretty soon the Negroes will be judges and doctors and mayors and professors and so forth. This fear of equality frightens them to death. It is a confession of deep-seated fear that, once the barrier of discriminatory laws and practices is removed, people of color will be found not only equal but ofttimes superior in ability. People of color are going to get equality of rights including the franchise. They are not only going to vote but hold positions of power and influence in legislatures, in courts, in education, in the professions, and in the business and financial world. They are going to provide some tough competition in the process. What a sorry state the semi-racists are going to be in when their suspicions are proved accurate and they can no longer look at a man of color and say "you are beneath me, your skin is a shade too dark."

If I had to stand before the bar of justice in defense of my freedom, life, or property, I would want the most learned, honorable, and wise man in the world on the bench, not the one with the whitest skin. The same would be true if life were ebbing away and a physician came to heal, or if I were to sit at the feet of a professor to learn the wisdom of the ages. The minds which have joined through the ages to give us civilization were not those of white men alone. Certainly many of the wise and good men among us are, always were, and always will be men of color. The annals of history are replete with their names and their contributions. Many of the most beautiful ornaments and artifacts in all the world came from the hands of their craftsmen. They have been statesmen, philosophers, scientists. No soldiers of the Union armies ever rejected them because of color, not when they came in the night to bring them food or lead them back to the Union lines. Not when they came by the thousands to save a nation which had so grievously oppressed them.

What is there about Europe's treatment of Africa over a period of 400 years to inspire trust and respect! Murder. Rapine. Enslavement. Colonialism. A robbery of millions of people of their freedom in their own homelands. What is there about our treatment of them to inspire trust and cooperation, let alone the love and respect upon which a democracy is so heavily dependent? We rejected them as a potential part of our cultural heritage. We subjected them to two hundred years of enslavement, and to another century of brutality and subordination. We did even worse. We tortured them with the charge of being an inferior people, and did everything we could to prove it. We placed it on the basis of color, a totally irrational bit of logic even if the charge had been true and a studied insult to about three-fourths of the people of the world.

Does anyone suppose that long continued slavery and persecution of the Negro could have survived in this country if there had been a national Negro state in Africa? That continent had so much room that it enjoyed a tribal, pastoral society, free from most of the savage competition of the industrial, urbanized Western World of today. It was in many respects a soul-satisfying, humane existence in comparison to our own; but it left the people helpless before the onslaught of European barbarism, and they fell prey to the slave traders and then to the exploiters of natural resources and the colonial dictators. Nationalism has now emerged in powerful form.

The Negro needed a homeland and he is getting it. Scholarship and emerging nationalism in Africa will soon give him a history reaching back to ancient times. They will not be the ancient times of white men; nor will the pride in their heritage be our pride. We may not even be able to comprehend it. We have lost the contribution Africa could have made to our culture. We probably have lost our great opportunity to assume leadership of the moral forces of the world. Had we put as much effort into promoting the welfare of all men as we did into submerging people of color, our leadership would now be established. We are on the defensive here, but refuse to face the fact or acknowledge the cause.

All of our money and fancy talk of themselves are not going to give us the support of other peoples. Our record at home is not good. It belies our pious statements of objectives. In the First World War, while vast numbers of our men of color were fighting in Europe to make the world safe for democracy, Negroes were being lynched and rioting against them was rampant at home. Then came the fanaticism of the Ku Klux Klan at the peak of its power. For one hundred years, any number of states and millions of people have denied the equality of men, in the crassest way possible, without refinements, making the nation appear hypocritical to the rest of the world. They used the law. They used mob violence. They used all kinds of economic pressures to subordinate people of color. They struck down universal manhood suffrage, appropriating to themselves the power and influence to which the oppressed were rightfully entitled. They gloried in their own fancied racial superiority. Now they close schools and libraries to keep children in ignorance. They imprison men of color and white men who sit down together to break bread. All of this belongs to totalitarianism, and it did not come from without. It has its roots down deep in the history of our country and the whole world knows it.

We are in the midst of world wide revolution, and neither force, nor fear, nor argument will stop this surge of masses of people for control of their own destiny. There is only one in way in which the United States can redeem democracy, guarantee its security, and regain the respect of the world. It is by a monumental act of retributive justice. New attitudes, new practices in our daily lives are necessary and inescapable in any case, but that is not enough. We can break down this almost impenetrable barrier to communication between the white man and the man of color; we can convince the entire world of our sincerity; we can build solidarity and strength in the nation; we can recover some of what we have lost by oppression; we can do all of these things and more by giving to every child of color the finest possible education and technical training at national expense, and never count the cost.

We do not urge this on the basis of giving special favors to people of color. We can never give them anything. Every thing we ever do for them will bear the indelible mark of retribution. We can not repair the damage done, nor recall our acts of cruelty, but we can lighten the punishment on the day of judgment by matching every lynching of the past with a Ph.D. of the future. There may well be other ways also of doing what needs to be done; but no nation can ever expect to recover its moral values by simply saying it is sorry. If its sorrow is deep enough to be lasting, it must entail more than lip-service to virtue.